P9-DTA-024

LITTLE
CAKES

LITTLE
CAKES

CLASSIC RECIPES FOR ANY OCCASION

Susan Waggoner

Illustrations by Sujean

Universe

First published in the United States of America in 2004
by UNIVERSE PUBLISHING
A Division of Rizzoli International Publications, Inc.
300 Park Avenue South
New York, NY 10010

www.rizzoliusa.com

2004 2005 2006 2007 / 10 9 8 7 6 5 4 3 2 1

Designer Jennifer Wagner
Publisher Charles Miers
Editor Christopher Steighner

Distributed in the U.S. trade by St. Martin's Press, New York

Printed in the United States of America

ISBN: 0-7893-1074-0
Library of Congress Control Number: 2003116731

LITTLE CAKES

HOW TO BAKE A CAKE

READING THE RECIPE

There's nothing worse than getting halfway through a recipe, time and ingredients already committed, and discovering something you've overlooked. Backtracking isn't just inconvenient—it can ruin your recipe. Cakes get their lightness from the air incorporated into them and from "quick rise" leavenings such as baking powder and baking soda. Once these chemical actions have been put in motion, you want to get the cake out of the mixing bowl and into the oven as swiftly as possible. Delays to locate missing ingredients or to review a skill are detrimental. The way to avoid this problem is to read the recipe all the way through at least once before you begin to bake. Also, turn on your oven before you start measuring and mixing.

MEASURING INGREDIENTS

Unless otherwise indicated, the measurements called for in this book are all intended to be level. When it comes to dry ingredients, this means you need dry ingredient measuring cups, not the lipped type, usually of glass, which is intended for liquids only. To get a level teaspoon, cup, or other measure of a dry ingredient, simply draw the straight, dull edge of a table knife across the top of your measure, letting the excess fall off. Note that brown sugar should be firmly packed— tamped down well enough that, when turned out, the sugar will hold its shape.

Always sift dry ingredients; sifting not only ensures accurate measuring, it also aerates and equally distributes ingredients. An ordinary kitchen strainer can be used in place of a sifter.

TIP Baking powder has a shelf life of about a year, after which it will become less active and produce disappointing results. To test the freshness of your baking powder, place 1 teaspoon in half a cup of hot water. If it doesn't bubble immediately, buy a new can. Similarly, baking soda can be tested in a small amount of vinegar.

A small, inexpensive food scale—the kind dieters are familiar with—is a very worthwhile investment, especially if you are going to bake with chocolate, which is measured by weight in recipes rather than volume.

TIP A pinch, as a measurement, is generally understood to be $1/16$ of a teaspoon, so if you have a $1/8$-teaspoon measuring spoon, you can estimate about half of that.

BRINGING INGREDIENTS TO ROOM TEMPERATURE

Recipe instructions that call for certain ingredients to be at room temperature should be taken seriously. Some people think this is just to make ingredients easier to blend. This is true, but the more important reason is that ingredients brought to room temperature make greater volume batter, and cakes that are higher and lighter.

BUTTER Butter is at room temperature when it yields easily to the touch but still holds its shape and is opaque. If the weather is warm on baking day, keep a close watch on your butter. To bring butter to room temperature quickly, place it in a bowl and set it in the oven with the oven light on and the oven door closed. (Don't set the bowl too close to the light or the butter may begin to melt.) Though the time needed will vary depending on the temperature in your kitchen and the size of your oven, I find that 15 to 20 minutes is usually enough to soften one stick (half a cup) of butter. Always use unsalted butter; since these recipes have been calibrated for unsalted butter, you will actually be adding more salt than needed if you use the salted variety.

EGGS Because cream whips best straight from the refrigerator, people sometimes think that cold is the operative ingredient in creating all whipped components. Not so. Eggs are easier to separate when they are cold, but egg whites whip best at room temperature. To quickly bring eggs to room temperature, place whole, uncracked eggs in a bowl of hot tap water for two minutes. Don't leave longer than that. Remove, dry shells with a paper towel, and use immediately.

MIXING INGREDIENTS

There are two general rules to follow when mixing ingredients. The first is to begin on a low speed and increase the speed after a few moments, when the initial mixing is well under way. This is especially important when adding flour to a creamed butter mixture, as a speed that is too high will send the flour flying out of the bowl. Once the flour has been incorporated into the butter, raise the speed to medium or medium-high. Eggs should also be incorporated in this way. Note that cake batter should never be beaten on your mixer's highest speed—that's for whipping cream and making meringues. The other rule to remember is to scrape down the sides of the bowl often. If you don't do this, some ingredients will not get properly mixed in, and some ingredients will be mixed longer than others.

Every cooking show diva has one: a big, beautiful, multi-horsepower KitchenAid mixer that dominates the counter. I have one too, but I didn't use it to test these recipes. Instead, I used the $12 handheld mixer I bought in a discount store several years ago. I wanted to make sure all the recipes in this book could be made without investing in an expensive piece of equipment, and I'm happy to report that they can be. For baking you do need an electric mixer of some kind, as it is too tedious and difficult to whip egg whites, cream, and the like by hand.

When choosing bowls for mixing, I prefer the stainless steel kind. Glass and crockery bowls are heavy and can be chipped by metal beaters. Plastic is the least desirable because minuscule amounts of fat can cling to even the cleanest plastic and ruin your meringue. With regard to shape, deep bowls are good because they confine spattering, and bowls with gently sloping sides are better for mixing than straight-sided, soufflé-style bowls.

WHIPPING EGG WHITES

First off, the American Egg Board warns against eating uncooked eggs. Although egg whites aren't nearly as likely to harbor bacteria as yolks are, they aren't risk free. Some of the fillings and frostings in this book call for whipped, uncooked whites. Meringue powder, available in baking shops and gourmet and grocery stores, is recommended as a substitute.

There seems to be a lot of intimidation hovering around the whipping of egg whites, and working with them after they are whipped. There's no need for this, so let's grab those beaters and go. Here's a simple, step-by-step guide to beating egg whites with a hand-held electric mixer:

* Make sure the bowl and beaters you're going to use are scrupulously clean and dry.
* Do not add other ingredients to egg whites until you reach the soft-peak stage (see below). Meringue forms more quickly when other ingredients aren't present.
* Begin at low speed and beat for about 10 seconds, until the whites begin to froth. Be sure to move the mixer around the bowl to incorporate all of the whites.
* Now increase the speed to medium. The whites will become very foamy and opaque. After 2 to 3 minutes, you will be at the soft-peak stage—that is, when the beater is lifted the whites will form a definite but non-rigid peak.
* As soon as the soft-peak stage is reached, increase the mixing speed to high and add (or begin adding) other ingredients if they are called for. The whites will become creamy and glossy. Test your progress by lifting the beater. When the whites form firm points whose tips stand straight up – stop! You have reached the stiff-peak stage.

* Do not beat egg whites beyond this point, or they will become clumpy and dry. And, while there are several alleged techniques for bringing back overbeaten whites, I've never found one that works reliably.

TIP To give your egg whites a boost and make them easier to whip, add a little cream of tartar when you reach the soft-peak stage, about $1/8$ teaspoon per egg white.

MELTING CHOCOLATE

The key words to remember when melting chocolate are low and slow. Chocolate burns easily, so too much heat will cause the drops that melted first to scorch while the rest hasn't even begun to soften. The optimum temperature is just high enough to melt the chocolate and keep it from resolidifying. Chocolate's other big enemy is water, and even a bit of steam can cause it to seize — that is, turn into a dull, stiff, grainy mass that is virtually impossible to work with.

Many people recommend melting chocolate in a microwave. I don't like doing anything in a microwave, and recommend melting chocolate over simmering water. If you have a double boiler, fine. If not, then place a saucepan of water over heat to simmer. Find a heatproof bowl that is big enough so that it rests on the rim of the saucepan without touching the water. Stainless steel mixing bowls are ideal. Stir the chocolate frequently as it melts, being sure to scrape down the sides of the bowl as the chocolate that gets caught there tends to cool and harden. Don't cover the chocolate at any point, as condensation may form, drip into the chocolate, and start the seizing process.

FOLDING INGREDIENTS

Folding is a technique used to blend delicate ingredients such as egg whites or whipped cream. It's a useful technique for all sorts of recipes and well worth learning to do correctly. Here's the step-by-step:
* Always fold by hand. An electric mixer is just too vigorous.
* The best tool for folding is a flat, paddle-type spatula whose wide blade is made of rubber or plastic and whose handle is made of plastic or wood. It's also essential for scraping down the sides of the bowl as you are mixing, and scraping the last bit of batter from the bowl to put into your cake pan.
* Understand that you are usually going to fold the more delicate ingredient into the less delicate ingredient, not the other way around. Let's say, for the purpose of this example, that your more delicate ingredient is egg whites. You add these to the bowl you have mixed your cake batter in.

9

* Make sure the bowl is large enough. You need room to work your spatula, and the batter should be shallow rather than deep.
* Before you begin adding the whites, give the batter a final stir and scrape down the sides of the bowl.
* Add about a quarter of the whites to the batter. With your spatula, stir the whites gently into the batter. This lightens the batter and will make it easier to incorporate the remaining whites.
* Now add the rest of the whites. With your spatula at the side of the bowl farthest from you, cut down through the batter and draw the spatula toward you, making a trough through both the batter and the egg whites with the wide blade of the spatula. Slide the spatula under the batter, as if it is a pancake turner; lift and turn, folding the heavier batter over the top of the egg whites.
* Give the bowl a quarter turn and repeat the step above. Scrape the sides of the bowl as needed. Keep turning and folding just until the whites are evenly distributed and no large clumps remain. Be careful not to over-blend or you will let too much air out of the whites.
* Try to work as swiftly as possible. It isn't easy at first, but once you've had a bit of practice you should be able to fold whites in a minute or less.

CHOOSING THE PAN

Once you have your batter mixed and ready to go, you need something to bake it in. Cake pans aren't expensive, and they're available almost everywhere,

from the grocery store to the local thrift shop. Most of them—whether of metal, glass, or that new, jelly-like material—are very good. The only pans I really don't like are the disposable aluminum foil ones, which are flimsy, and easy to bend, pierce, and spill. Buy something lasting instead.

The vast majority of cakes in this book are formulated to be made in 8-inch round pans. I prefer 8-inch to 9-inch for small cakes, as an 8-inch pan produces a thicker layer that can be cut into two layers if you wish to use a filling. If you only want to buy one cake pan in your life, I recommend an 8-inch springform, as it will do double duty for both regular cakes and cheesecakes. (One of the advantages of homemade cakes is that the batter is thicker and won't drip through a springform pan, as a cake mix batter would.) Another good size to have on hand is an 8-inch square pan, though if you don't have a pan this size you can still make cake requiring one; just use an 8-inch round pan and use the excess batter to make a few cupcakes. If you have a 6-inch round springform pan, you can use it to make two small layers in place of one 8-inch round layer.

Note that all pans are not created equal. In addition to coming in eccentric sizes, pans theoretically of the same size can vary from manufacturer to manufacturer. When you make a cake, note for future reference how the finished product fared in the pan you used.

Of course, if you want to go pan crazy, there is almost an infinite variety of pans and molds you can buy; however, you can avoid much of this expense by looking around your kitchen for items you already own. I've baked in many things, including:
BREAD PANS There's a whole chapter on loaf cakes in this book, and almost any recipe for an 8-inch round cake will fit in one large or two small loaf pans.
CASSEROLE DISHES If you can bake a tuna casserole in it, you can make a cake in it.
CAST-IRON SKILLETS Upside-down cakes were originally known as skillet cakes for good cause. A well-seasoned cast-iron skillet is a joy to bake in.
CUSTARD CUPS AND RAMEKINS These are both ideal for baking small individual cakes.

TIP A clear heatproof glass item that comes in a set of four and is labeled a "custard cup" will cost less than a dollar. Call it a ramekin, make it out of crockery, and sell it individually, and it will cost five times as much.

JELLO MOLDS One of the things I inherited from my mother's kitchen was a set of individual-serving size aluminum 1950s-era jello molds in the shape of hearts, stars, and fluted domes. I've baked in them lots of times with good results. Just remember to avoid molds that are too detailed, as the cake batter will stick in the intricate little crevices, even if you have done a good job of greasing and flouring.
SOUFFLÉ DISHES This is another ovenproof dish that lends itself well to cake baking. In fact, I discovered one of my favorite cheesecake tricks using a soufflé dish: bake the cake in the soufflé dish set in a larger pan filled with an inch or so of water. The warm, steaming water will give the cheesecake a wonderfully creamy quality. (To get the cheesecake out, invert it onto a plate, then invert again onto another plate, to get it right side up.)
TIN CANS My grandmother, who was born in 1886, taught me this one. Back in the days when orange juice concentrate came in real tin cans, she used to make the most charming little quick breads in them. Taking a cue from her, I have a collection of "cake pans" that started life as tuna fish cans and are just right for baking individual mini-cakes. The cans aren't deep, so you can't fill them very full—just $\frac{1}{4}$ to $\frac{1}{3}$ cup of batter in each. Since the bottoms of these cans usually have an indented ring pattern, be sure to line the bottom of each with a circle of wax paper or parchment, so that you will have a smooth surface.

TIP A good way to determine whether or not your cake will fit into a non-standard pan is to estimate the surface area of the pan and compare it to the area of the pan the recipe calls for.

PREPARING THE PAN

Please, please, please: don't use anything that comes in an aerosol can to do this, unless you are really fond of the taste of aerosol cans. Use butter, margarine, or vegetable shortening smeared on a bit of waxed paper or, if you unwrapped a stick of butter to make your cake, use the paper the butter was wrapped in. Gloss the pan lightly, making sure to get the corners and crevices. Now sprinkle a spoonful or so of flour into the pan. Tilt and pat the pan to distribute the flour, making sure the sides, bottom, corners, and crevices are coated. Now turn the pan upside down over the sink and tap it briskly to remove excess flour—there's nothing less appetizing than getting a piece of cake with a large, damp clump of flour clinging to it.

Some recipes call for lining the cake pan with parchment or waxed paper. To make a liner for your pan, simply set it on the paper and trace around it. Cut out a little to the inside of your outline (to make sure the liner isn't too big) and place in the bottom of your pan.

When you're ready to bake, pour the batter into the prepared pan. "Pour" may not quite be technically accurate, since cake batter made from scratch is thicker than cake mix batters. The good news is you don't have to worry about raisins, nuts, or chocolate chips sinking to the bottom. The bad news is if you don't watch what you're doing, you may end up with air pockets. When you turn your batter into the pan, be sure to spread it well, right up to the edges of the pan.

Take a moment to smooth the top as well, as a cake that isn't level when it goes into the oven will bake unevenly.

TIP What's the difference between parchment and wax paper? About $5 a roll. Another difference is that you probably already have waxed paper in your kitchen, and would need to go out and buy parchment. Whichever you happen to have, use it; there is very little performance difference.

BAKING TIME & TEMPERATURE

Yes, even ovens require a bit of know-how. Here are some tips for the baking stage:
* Oven thermometers are helpful but not vital, and two ovens can register the same temperature and produce different results. More important than any oven thermometer is to learn the quirks of your oven and make the necessary adjustments in setting the time and temperature.
* People often underestimate the time it takes to preheat thoroughly. For most ovens, half an hour is required to ensure full heat.

⁎ Keeping the oven at an even temperature throughout is important. Don't open the door at all for the first 15 minutes, and if you must peek after that, make it quick.

⁎ If you have the oven light on, be aware that this will raise the temperature somewhat.

⁎ Position your cake in the middle of the oven unless a recipe specifically tells you not to. "Middle" means not only front to back and side to side but up and down.

⁎ If you are baking something else on another shelf, stagger the pans so they do not line up directly above and below each other. Staggering permits a more even flow of heat.

⁎ If you are using glass or dark metal pans, decrease oven temperature by approximately 25 degrees.

⁎ If you are trying a recipe for the first time, set the oven timer a few minutes on the short side. In case the time is wrong for your oven, you'll get to your cake before it burns.

TESTING FOR DONENESS

A cake is done when it develops a slightly browned crust, and the sides begin to pull away slightly from the pan. If you press your fingertip lightly to the dome, the cake should spring back, making the indentation fade. A cake tester is also a reliable aid: when it is inserted into the center of the cake, it should come out clean, free of batter or liquid. In the old days, women used broomstraws to test the doneness of their cakes. Then came the hygiene-minded modern age and metal cake testers appeared everywhere. Well, the pioneer girls had it right. Metal testers are unreliable because the thin metal filament heats up so quickly it can cause still-quaking batter to slide off it, leaving the impression that a cake is done when it actually isn't. Bamboo skewers work well.

COOLING AND UNMOLDING

Cakes made in square pans are usually meant to be frosted in the pan and served from it. While you can treat round cakes the same way, they are usually meant to be unmolded and placed on a serving plate.

Many cookbooks call for you to remove the cake from the pan as soon as possible and finish cooling it on a wire rack. The directions in this book don't call for this because, while racks are fine, I've discovered the downside often outweighs the benefit. Cakes removed from their pans are very vulnerable and prone to accident and drying out. Since most cakes can cool happily in their pans, cooling racks are far from a necessity. Just don't make the mistake of setting it on the stove to cool—the heat of the stove will keep the baking process going, and that isn't what you want. Also, never cover a cake until it has cooled completely, as the condensation will cause problems.

TIP I like to bake in springform pans—they are so easy to unmold.

To unmold, begin with a cake that has cooled completely. Using a metal spatula or table knife, run the blade completely around the edge of the pan to make sure the cake is loose. If you were ambitious enough to make a liner for the bottom of the pan, you're ready for the next step. If you didn't line the pan, gently slide the tip of the blade under the edge of the cake to loosen. Do this in a few places and the cake should come free. If not, try the same approach with a small pancake turner. Be patient and your cake will come free. Never proceed to unmold a cake that still has parts sticking to the pan, as the chances of the stuck part tearing and remaining in the pan are large.

When your cake is loosened, have two large flat plates ready, an ordinary plate and the plate you mean to serve the cake on. Place the ordinary plate face down on the pan. Invert so that the cake is upside down on the plate. Quickly place the serving plate over the cake and invert again. Now your cake is right side up on your serving plate.

Once you have unmolded your cake, frost it immediately, cover it with plastic wrap, or transfer it to a storage container, as cake dries out quickly. In fact, the key purpose of frosting is to seal the cake and protect it from the drying air.

CUTTING A ONE-LAYER CAKE INTO TWO LAYERS

I love cutting a small, one-layer cake into two layers. It gives you more surface to fill or frost and gives a humble cake elegance. To do this, make sure your cake is completely cooled. You will need a long, serrated knife and a flat, even surface to work on. The first thing to do is decide where to cut. If your cake is perfectly flat, make the horizonatl cut halfway up the side of the cake, parallel to the work surface. However, if your cake has a high dome, make the cut higher up the side, so that the bottom and the top will appear more equal. Begin cutting with the knife blade parallel to the counter. Place your free hand firmly on the top of the cake to prevent sliding and shifting. Cut straight across with a gentle sawing motion, keeping the blade level and continuing to gently hold the cake from the top.

STORING CAKES

The trick to keeping leftover cake tasting as good the second day as it did the first is proper storage. While icebox cakes and cakes that have whipped cream frosting must be kept in the refrigerator, other varieties are best kept at room temperature. Covering a cake with plastic wrap or foil has a few disadvantages. Aside from sticking to the frosting and making a mess, these coverings aren't airtight and can still result in drying. The best storage is a Tupperware-style container, large enough to accommodate both the cake and its serving plate, and deep enough that the lid easily clears the top of the cake.

TROUBLESHOOTING

It happens to everyone sometime: a cake just goes wrong. Instead of rising it sinks into a soggy mess. Or you cut into it and discover large, tunnel-like holes. I've had my share of these failures, especially when experimenting with cakes for this book.

What do you do when a cake flops? The first thing to do is taste it. Does it taste good? Surprisingly, most failed cakes do taste good—it's the shape or the texture that leaves something to be desired. If you don't like the taste at all, drop the cake from your repertoire. In my experience, taste isn't related to the failure, so if you don't care for the cake it's probably not worth fussing over. If you do like the cake, however, eat it anyway with some creative fixes. Cakes with slightly sunken tops are all the rage right now, indicating an abundance of rich, dense ingredients. Or fill the dent with a bit of extra frosting. When I overfilled some ramekins with chocolate batter, resulting in sunken and somewhat gooey centers, I used a spoon to enhance the hollow, put a scoop of ice cream in each, and called it Ice Cream In Cake. If a cake tastes good but is simply too ugly to dress up, break it into chunks and make Trifle (page 81).

Besides rescuing my failed cake, I try to remake a successful version right away. If I don't, I know I will always avoid that particular recipe, probably for no good reason. So it's a bit like getting back on a horse after you've fallen. Of course, it helps if you have some idea why your cake went wrong. The most common reasons for cake failure include not paying attention to the recipe, making freelance substitutions to the recipe, having an insufficiently heated oven, and using a wrong size pan.

USEFUL SUBSTITUTIONS

1 cup cake flour =
1 cup minus 2 tablespoons all-purpose flour

1 cup all-purpose flour =
1 cup plus 2 tablespoons cake flour

1 cup milk =
1/2 cup evaporated milk plus 1/2 cup water

2 large eggs = 3 small eggs

1/2 cup butter = 1/2 cup firm margarine or
**1/2 cup minus 1 tablespoon solid shortening
(Do not use ultra creamy butter or
butter-flavored shortening)**

1 teaspoon baking powder =
1/2 teaspoon cream of tartar plus 1/4 teaspoon baking soda plus 1/4 teaspoon cornstarch

1 tablespoon cornstarch = 2 tablespoons flour

1 ounce unsweetened chocolate =
3 tablespoons unsweetened cocoa powder plus 1 tablespoon butter or margarine

1 ounce semisweet chocolate =
1/2 ounce unsweetened chocolate plus 1 tablespoon sugar

1/2 cup brown sugar=
6 tablespoons granulated sugar plus 2 tablespoons molasses

1/2 cup sour cream = 1/2 cup yogurt

WHITE AND YELLOW CAKES

Many people think that the white flour needed to produce the light, fine-grained cakes of today is a fairly recent invention. It isn't. White flour was known to the Romans as early as 150 B.C., and patrician Romans not only preferred but insisted on white bread to eat. The status-conscious Victorians were particularly fond of white flour, even though they realized it was not as nutritious as its darker and more robust counterparts. The time-intensive process of crushing and sieving the grain made it expensive and desirable. Hand in hand with a love of white flour went a love of the light, fine-grained cakes it could create. Humbler households served brown bread and butter, or less expensive treats like gingerbread, whose sturdiness lent itself to the use of heavier flours.

All this began to change in 1834, with the invention of the rollermill. Slowly, the new mills began replacing the grindstones of old, and by the 1870s the production of white flour at reasonable prices was economically profitable for the first time in history. Now ordinary people could enjoy the types of cakes the wealthy had been eating for years. Since the vestiges of status still clung to white flour, housewives took a special pride in using it. From the mid-1800s on, there was a boom in white and yellow cakes, whose very color proved the worth of the ingredients involved.

SILVER CAKE

When I first began reading and collecting old cookbooks, I was enchanted by the frequent appearance of recipes for Silver Cake, and became very interested in its origins. I eventually discovered that the Silver Cakes I'd found, dating from the 1930s and 1940s, were altered descendants of the original version, which dates from the pre-baking-powder days of the nineteenth century. Originally, this cake was similar to angel food except that, in addition to a high volume of egg whites, it also used butter. One of the first published recipes for Silver Cake comes from *What Mrs. Fisher Knows about Old Southern Cooking*, the first American cookbook by an ex-slave, published in 1881. Abby Fisher's recipe called for a dozen egg whites, a pound of butter, and a pound of powdered sugar, all of which were beaten together with a little milk, almond extract, and yeast until very light. When baking powder came along later in the century, people weren't willing to part with their Silver Cake recipes. Instead, they adapted them to the new invention, using fewer egg whites in combination with baking powder. If you have never tried this cake before, you should—it has a special, delicate lightness that's hard to resist.

1 cup sifted cake flour
1 teaspoon baking powder
Pinch of salt
3 tablespoons plus 2 teaspoons unsalted butter, at room temperature
2/3 cup sugar
1/2 teaspoon vanilla extract
1/3 cup milk
2 large egg whites
PAN 8-INCH ROUND PAN, GREASED.

1 Place the flour, baking powder, and salt in a bowl. Stir to combine and set aside.
2 In a mixing bowl, cream the butter, sugar, and vanilla until light and fluffy.
3 Alternately add the dry ingredients and milk, beating well after each addition.
4 In a separate bowl, beat the egg whites until stiff. Gently fold into the cake batter and turn into the prepared pan.
5 Bake at 350 degrees for 28 to 33 minutes.

PRESENTATION Powdered Sugar Glaze (see page 101) goes well with this cake. For a more spectacular finish, however, try a white icing such as the Basic Vanilla Frosting on page 96, liberally garnished with toasted coconut.

PERFECT WHITE CAKE

During the nouvelle cuisine frenzy of the 1970s and 80s, white cake was a rare and much-maligned treat. Taking its place on menus were upstarts with names like Mango Torte Imperiale and Triple Mocha Molten Chocolate Mud Slide. Brides-to-be threw over long-standing tradition and opted for wedding cakes of carrot and carob chip. Well! Thank goodness that particular little reign of terror is over, and white cake stands tall once again. The truth is, there are few cakes as delectable—or as versatile—as a properly-made white cake.

2 large egg whites

$^3/_4$ teaspoon vanilla

$^1/_2$ cup milk, at room temperature

1 $^1/_2$ cups sifted cake flour

2 teaspoons baking powder

$^1/_4$ teaspoon salt

$^3/_4$ cup sugar

$^1/_4$ cup plus 2 tablespoons unsalted butter, at room temperature

PAN 8-INCH ROUND PAN, GREASED AND FLOURED.

1 Combine the egg whites, vanilla, and 2 tablespoons of the milk. Stir lightly and set aside.

2 In a mixing bowl, combine the flour, baking powder, salt, and sugar. Stir to combine thoroughly. Add the butter and remaining milk. Stir to combine, and then beat for about 2 minutes. Add half of the egg mixture and beat well. Repeat with remaining half. Pour into the prepared pan and bake at 350 degrees for approximately 30 minutes.

PRESENTATION I especially like this cake with Decorator Icing (page 96), which makes it taste like a traditional wedding cake. But you can frost it with almost any icing of your choice.

TIP If you want to make your white cake as white as possible, use bleached flour and replace the $^3/_4$ teaspoon vanilla with $^1/_2$ teaspoon clear almond extract.

Coconut Cake

Mix 1 cup shredded coconut into the Perfect White Cake batter before pouring into the cake pan. If you want to recapture the joy of a favorite candy bar, top with a thin icing of chocolate glaze and garnish with toasted slivered almonds.

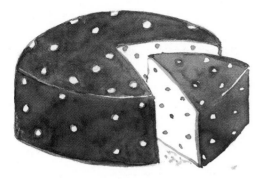

Chocolate Chip Cake

Mix 1 cup chocolate chips or mini chocolate chips into the Perfect White Cake batter before pouring into the cake pan.

Lady Baltimore Cake

This cake became a sensation when novelist Owen Wister served it up in his Southern novel of the same name. To make this belle of a cake, cut a cooled Perfect White Cake into two layers. Toss together 1/2 cup raisins, 1/3 cup coarsely chopped pecans or walnuts, 1/3 cup chopped candied cherries, and 2 teaspoons sherry, amaretto or vanilla extract. Make Lady Baltimore Frosting (page 95) and transfer half to a separate bowl. Gently fold half of the fruit and nut mixture into half of the frosting and spread on the bottom half of the cake. Cover with the top half of the cake. Spread the remaining frosting over the top, and arrange the remaining fruit–nut mixture around the edge in a decorative ring. To make an updated version of this recipe, include 1/2 cup coconut in the fruit–nut mix.

Strawberry Cream Cake

Clean and stem 1 pint of fresh strawberries. Select 4 nicely shaped berries and reserve as a garnish. Cut remaining berries into quarters, sprinkle with a little sugar, and set aside. Make a double batch of Whipped Cream (page 93) and set in the refrigerator until ready for use. Cut a cooled Perfect White Cake into two layers. Arrange the quartered berries over the bottom half of the cake, spooning on a bit of juice between the berries. Spread half of the whipped cream over the berries. Place the top half back on cake and spread with the remaining whipped cream. Cut the 4 reserved berries in half and arrange, compass-point style, on the whipped cream. Like all cakes with whipped cream, this must be stored in the refrigerator. This cake is also good with fresh whole raspberries.

WHITE CHOCOLATE CAKE

The addition of white chocolate, cream, and sour cream makes this cake subtly rich and just right for a special occasion.

1 1/4 cups cake flour
1 1/2 teaspoons baking powder
Pinch of salt
1/4 cup heavy cream
1/4 cup sour cream

3 ounces white chocolate
1/2 cup unsalted butter, at room temperature
3/4 cup sugar
1/2 teaspoon vanilla extract
2 large eggs, separated
PAN 8-OR 9-INCH ROUND PAN, GREASED AND FLOURED.

1 Sift the measured flour, baking powder, and salt together into a bowl and set aside.
2 Whisk the cream and sour cream together and set aside.
3 Melt the chocolate over simmering water. Set aside to let cool.
4 Cream the butter and 1/2 cup of the sugar together until light and fluffy.
5 Stir the vanilla into chocolate, and mix into butter mixture.
6 Add the egg yolks one at a time, mixing well after each addition.
7 Add half of the dry ingredients, then half of cream and sour cream, mixing well after each addition. Repeat with remaining half of ingredients.
8 Beat the egg whites until soft peaks form. Gradually add the remaining 1/4 cup sugar, beating continuously until stiff but not dry.
9 Fold the beaten egg whites into the batter, then turn into prepared pan. Bake at 350 degrees for 35 to 40 minutes.

PRESENTATION This cake is beautiful with White Chocolate Meringue or White Chocolate Almond Buttercream (page 99) and a scattering of fresh berries, chocolate curls, or both. It's equally good with the Chocolate Meringue Frosting on page 100 or a good chocolate glaze or ganache.

White Chocolate Apricot Cake

Cut the cooled White Chocolate Cake into two layers. Spread the bottom layer with Apricot Glaze (page 106). Replace top and frost with your choice of frostings. Garnish with chopped toasted hazelnuts.

Coconut Almond White Chocolate Cake

Replace the vanilla extract with $1/4$ teaspoon almond extract. Add $1/2$ cup coconut and $1/2$ cup chopped roasted almonds to the White Chocolate Cake batter before folding in the egg whites. Frost with your choice of frostings.

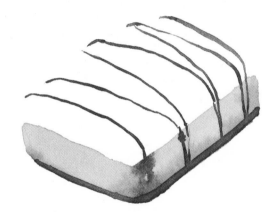

White Chocolate Lemon Cake

Replace the vanilla extract with $1/2$ teaspoon lemon extract, and add 1 to 2 teaspoons (to taste) grated lemon zest to the White Chocolate Cake batter before folding in the egg whites. When the cake is cool, slice into two layers and cover the bottom half with Lemon Curd Filling (page 106) or Lemon Syrup (page 106). Garnish frosted cake with lemon Candied Citrus Curls (page 91).

ANGEL CUPS

No one ever asks where angel food got its name—it's perfectly clear that this light and cloud-like cake is straight from heaven, the stuff angels really might dine on. Where and how it originated, however, is another matter. Many insist it's an invention of the Pennsylvania Dutch, whose thrifty housewives sought a use for the many egg whites leftover from making egg noodles. Another theory gives the honor to African-American cooks, since the cake was a favorite at their funeral luncheons. Still another possibility is the Missouri woman who made it as a

specialty of the house for the Beer Hotel in St. Louis in the 1880s. Who exactly deserves the honor remains uncertain, but the cake seemed to appear in all these venues in the mid-to-late 1800s, and spread rapidly across the continent. These are very good, and so light they almost float off your palm.

¼ cup sifted cake flour
6 tablespoons sugar
3 large egg whites, at room temperature
Pinch of salt
¼ teaspoon cream of tartar
¼ teaspoon vanilla extract
A few drops almond extract
PAN STANDARD MUFFIN TIN LINED WITH
9 TO 10 PAPER BAKING CUPS.

1 In a small bowl, combine the flour and 3 tablespoons of the sugar. Whisk to combine and to incorporate some air into the ingredients. Set aside.
2 If you have a metal mixing bowl, be sure to use it; make sure it is completely clean, dry, and free of traces of grease or oil. Transfer the egg whites to this bowl and beat at low speed until the whites begin to foam.

TIP This recipe can also be made with thawed frozen egg whites or meringue powder equivalent to 3 egg whites. (If using frozen egg whites, measure $\frac{1}{2}$ cup of whites).

3 Add the salt and cream of tartar and increase the speed to medium, beating until the whites are opaque and mound softly, like sheets billowing in the wind. Still on medium, beat in the remaining sugar gradually, 1 tablespoon at a time. The meringue will be very shiny and should form soft peaks. If not, beat a bit longer.

4 Add the vanilla and almond extracts and beat just enough to blend.

5 Sift the dry ingredients onto meringue gradually, 1 to 2 tablespoons at a time, folding gently after each addition.

6 Using a serving spoon, drop the batter into the cups. Since this batter is extremely light and won't necessarily "settle" on its own, it's easy to get large air pockets. Use the spoon to distribute the batter as you drop it in. Also, smooth down any topknots on the surface, since these will only scorch during baking.

7 Bake at 325 degrees for 18 to 20 minutes. You do not need to remove the Angel Cups from the paper baking cups.

PRESENTATION Powdered Sugar Glaze (page 101) or any other light frosting is perfect for Angel Cups. You can also enjoy them plain, or split them in half and fill them with whipped cream and fresh fruit.

VARIATIONS
You can change the flavor of Angel Cups by increasing the amount of almond extract and decreasing the vanilla, or by replacing the vanilla with orange or lemon extracts. Don't use orange or lemon juices to build flavor, as the amount needed will distort the delicate balance of ingredients.

1 Measure the flour, baking powder, and salt into a bowl. Stir to combine and set aside.
2 In a mixing bowl, cream the butter until light and fluffy. Add the sugar and beat until thoroughly blended. Beat in the eggs one at a time. Blend in the vanilla.
3 Add the dry ingredients alternately with milk, one-half of each at a time, mixing just until blended and smooth and creamy.
4 Spread in prepared pan and bake at 350 degrees, 25 to 30 minutes.

EVERYDAY YELLOW CAKE

Who can resist a tender yellow cake topped with creamy chocolate frosting? This buttery yellow cake is as easy as it gets.

1 ½ cups sifted cake flour
1 ½ teaspoons baking powder
¼ teaspoon salt
½ cup unsalted butter, at room temperature
1 cup sugar
2 large eggs, at room temperature
1 teaspoon vanilla extract
½ cup milk
PAN 8-OR 9-INCH ROUND PAN, GREASED AND FLOURED.

PRESENTATION Frost with a chocolate frosting or, for an extra treat, make a double batch of frosting, slice the cake into two layers, and fill and frost with chocolate.

Boston Cream Pie

Credit for inventing this dessert—which was never a pie in the first place—goes to a French chef who is said to have created it for the opening of Boston's Parker House Hotel in 1856. The original was made with a sponge cake base, but the moister yellow cake has replaced it as the standard. For the trivia-minded among you, Boston Cream Pie has been the official dessert of the state of Massachusetts since 1996. To make, cut a cooled Everyday Yellow Cake horizontally to make two layers.

Spread Vanilla Custard Filling (page 105) on the bottom half. Replace top half of cake and frost with Buttery Chocolate Glaze (page 98).

Washington's Birthday Cake

Nowadays, Presidents' Day is just another sale day. But back in the days when the first American president had a holiday all to himself, February 22 never went by without a flurry of cherry desserts. Before you begin your cake, make one batch of the Bing or Sour Cherry Filling on page 105 and let it cool. Swirl half of the topping into the batter for Everyday Yellow Cake and bake according to directions above. Top cooled cake with remaining filling and serve with whipped cream.

Blueberry Swirl Cake

Follow same method as Washington's Birthday Cake, above, using Blueberry Filling on page 105. Serve with whipped cream or dot with dollops of Lemon Curd Filling (page 106).

Better Than Sex Cake

This is a new classic, although a few different types of cakes seem to be competing for the title. I've adapted the recipe to make the cake truly "from scratch." It is indeed delicious—whether or not it's actual ly better than sex depends on the kind of life you lead. Prepare a cooled Everyday Yellow Cake by poking several holes into the top with a drinking straw, pen, or pencil. In a saucepan, combine 10 ounces of crushed pineapple and juice (half of a large can) with $1/4$ cup sugar. Heat to boiling, stirring to dissolve the sugar. Cook for about 5 minutes, stirring frequently. Spread over the top of the cake, making sure some of the syrup drips into the holes. Allow to cool. Make one recipe Whipped Cream (page 93) and spread over cooled pineapple topping. Garnish with $1/2$ cup toasted coconut and $1/2$ cup pecans, broken in pieces. Some recipes also call for banana slices. If you wish to add them, don't do so until immediately before serving, as they darken very quickly.

GOLD CAKE

This sunshine-yellow cake dates from a century ago, when every farm wife had eggs to spare and no one worried about cholesterol. In fact, you can chart society's shifting demographics—from rural to urban to cholesterol-conscious—by the changes in this cake. Cookbooks I have from the 1920s frequently call for eight egg yolks for a two-layer cake, while cookbooks of the 1940s and 50s make do with five or six.

3 large egg yolks
1 teaspoon vanilla extract
1 1/3 cups sifted cake flour
1 3/4 teaspoons baking powder
Pinch of salt
3/4 cup sugar
1/4 cup plus 2 tablespoons unsalted butter, at room temperature

1/4 cup plus 2 tablespoons milk
1 large egg white

PAN 9-INCH ROUND PAN OR 8- OR 9-INCH SQUARE PAN, GREASED AND FLOURED. (OR USE AN 8-INCH ROUND PAN AND REMOVE ENOUGH BATTER TO MAKE THREE OR FOUR CUPCAKES.)

1 In a bowl, beat the egg yolks and vanilla until thick and light. Set aside.
2 In a mixing bowl, combine the flour, baking powder, salt, and sugar. Stir to combine. Add the butter and milk. Stir to combine, then beat for about 2 minutes.
3 Add the egg yolks in two batches, beating well after each addition.
4 In a separate bowl, beat the egg white until stiff but not dry. Fold gently into batter.
5 Pour the batter into prepared pan and bake at 350 degrees for 25 to 30 minutes.

PRESENTATION As with Everyday Yellow Cake, this one is spectacular with a chocolate frosting. Don't be afraid to branch out, though: Orange Buttercream, Lemon Buttercream, and Butter Pecan (pages 99 and 103) are all delightful on this cake.

TIP Don't throw away those extra egg whites; freeze them. You can defrost them later to make either the Perfect White Cake on page 18 or the Angel Cups on page 22.

Daffodil Cake

A few types of yellow cake, ranging from sponge to angel food to gold, bear this name, depending on the vintage of the cookbook you are looking at. Some are a mix of white and yellow batters and others, like this one, involve dressing the cake with a daffodil-hued lemon filling and frosting. Cut a cooled Gold Cake horizontally to make two layers. Spread Lemon Curd Filling (page 106) on the bottom. Replace the top half of the cake and frost top with Lemon Buttercream Frosting (page 99).

Golden Apricot Cake

Cut a cooled Gold Cake horizontally to make two layers. Spread bottom half with Apricot Glaze (page 106). Replace the top half of the cake and frost top with Coffee Buttercream Frosting (page 99).

Lord Baltimore Cake

Chances are better than even that neither Lord Baltimore nor the city that bears his name had anything to do with the origins of this cake. Like the Lady Baltimore Cake on page 19, the recipe seems to be a southern one, and probably earned its name by being the fair lady's counterpart, using egg yolks rather than whites. To make this cake, cut a cooled Gold Cake into two layers and set aside. Make Lady Baltimore Frosting on page 95 and divide in half. To one-half of the frosting add $1/4$ cup crushed macaroon crumbs, $1/4$ cup coarsely chopped pecans, and $1/4$ cup drained and chopped maraschino cherries. Mix well and spread onto the bottom half of the cake. Replace the top and spread with the remaining frosting. Garnish with a border of additional cherries alternated with pecan halves.

GENOISE

Though many think of it as the ultimate French sponge cake, Genoise is named in honor of its home city, Genoa, Italy. What makes this cake different is not the ingredients involved but the method in which it is made, in which the eggs are warmed and beaten and the butter is added last.

1/4 cup unsalted butter

3 large eggs

1/2 cup sugar

3/4 teaspoon almond extract (if you do not like almond, replace with 1 teaspoon vanilla extract)

1/2 cup all-purpose flour

PAN 8-INCH ROUND OR, IF THE CAKE IS TO BE CUT INTO PETIT FOURS (PAGE 74), 8- OR 9-INCH SQUARE. PREPARE PAN BY CUTTING WAX PAPER LINER TO FIT BOTTOM. GREASE THE WAX PAPER AND SIDES OF THE PAN.

1 Melt the butter and set aside to cool.

2 In a heatproof bowl, beat the eggs lightly. Stir in the sugar.

3 Fill a saucepan with 1 to 2 inches warm water and place over very low heat. Set the egg bowl over the saucepan. Make sure water does not get hot enough to simmer. Bring the egg mixture to lukewarm temperature, stirring frequently.

4 Remove the bowl from the heat and beat the eggs on high for 3 minutes. Add the almond extract. Beat for another 3 to 4 minutes, until thick and lemon-yellow.

5 Sift one-fourth of flour over batter and fold in. Repeat until all the flour has been added.

6 Fold in the cooled, melted butter.

7 Pour the batter in the pan and bake at 350 degrees for 20 to 25 minutes.

PRESENTATION This is a light, versatile cake that is made to be dressed up, and the variety of finishing touches is almost infinite. You can cut the cake in half horizontally and fill with almost any frosting, glaze, filling, jam, or fruit puree. Or brush with a little liqueur or Lemon Syrup (page 106).

Chocolate Genoise

Melt 1 1/2 ounces semisweet chocolate with the butter and follow method above.

Lemon Genoise

Replace the almond extract with 1 teaspoon of lemon extract. Add 1 teaspoon grated lemon zest with the melted butter.

Orange Genoise

Replace the almond extract with 1 tablespoon of orange juice. Add 1 teaspoon grated orange zest with the melted butter.

Hazelnut Genoise

Fold in 3 1/2 ounces ground hazelnuts in batches as you fold in the flour.

29

WHIPPED CREAM CAKE

This cake is similar to silver cake but, as the name implies, has the added fillip of rich whipped cream.

1 cup sifted cake flour
$^1/_4$ teaspoon salt
1 $^1/_4$ teaspoons baking powder
2 large egg whites
$^1/_4$ cup heavy cream
$^3/_4$ cup sugar
$^1/_4$ cup cold water
$^1/_2$ teaspoon vanilla extract
$^1/_2$ teaspoon almond extract

PAN 8-INCH ROUND PAN, PREPARED BY LINING THE BOTTOM WITH WAX PAPER.

1 Measure the sifted flour, salt, and baking powder together in a bowl. Stir to combine and set aside.
2 In a mixing bowl, beat the egg whites until stiff but not dry or clumpy.
3 In a separate bowl, beat cream until stiff. Gently fold the whipped cream into the beaten egg whites.
4 Add sugar gradually, mixing to combine thoroughly.
5 Add the dry ingredients alternately with the water, a quarter of each at a time, mixing carefully.
6 Add the flavorings and blend well. Pour into the prepared pan and bake at 350 degrees for 25 to 30 minutes.

PRESENTATION Frost with frosting of your choice and, if you wish, fresh berries or pecan slices.

CHEESECAKE CAKE

I found the basis for this recipe in a vintage booklet published by the Peavey milling company of Minneapolis. I was curious to try it as it seemed new and different, despite being old. The results were so good that my neighbor, who acts as my taster, showed up the next day demanding more. How this cake missed becoming a classic I'll never know.

For the cake:

1 cup all-purpose flour
1 teaspoon baking powder
1/2 teaspoon salt
1/4 cup unsalted butter, at room temperature
2/3 cup sugar
1 teaspoon vanilla extract
1/2 cup milk

For the topping:

8 ounces cream cheese, at room temperature
1/4 cup milk
2 large eggs
1/3 cup sugar
PAN 8-OR 9-INCH SQUARE PAN, GREASED AND FLOURED.

Make the cake:

1 Combine the flour, baking powder, and salt. Stir to combine and set aside.
2 In a mixing bowl, cream the butter, sugar, and vanilla until light.
3 Add the dry ingredients alternately with milk, half at a time, beating well after each addition.
4 Spread the batter in the prepared pan.

Make the topping:

1 Cream the cheese until smooth and blend in the milk. Add the eggs one at a time, then the sugar. Mix to blend thoroughly, then pour over the top of the cake batter.
2 Bake at 350 degrees for 35 to 40 minutes.

PRESENTATION This cake is excellent on its own, garnished with Candied Citrus Curls (page 91), or with a sprinkle of nutmeg. You can also serve it, as you would a cheesecake, with a helping of fruit or a fruit sauce or topping.

CHOCOLATE CAKES

It took a surprisingly long time for two made-for-each-other foods — cake and chocolate — to meet and marry. Although chocolate was imported into Europe as early as the mid-sixteenth century, it was enjoyed strictly as a beverage until the nineteenth century. The first edible chocolate bar wasn't produced until 1847, ushering in a golden age for chocolate lovers, as chocolate became progressively less expensive, higher in quality, and spun into ever more delicious confections. This is when chocolate began to gain popularity as a cake ingredient. Many early recipes for "chocolate cake" actually refer to white or yellow cake frosted with chocolate, and the first all-chocolate cakes seem to have been prepared by professional or royal chefs for an elite clientele. However, as the price of chocolate continued to moderate, more and more middle-class homemakers found it within reach. Fudge was a popular home-made treat, and by the end of the nineteenth century recipes for chocolate-based cakes were becoming increasingly common.

EASY LAVA CUPS

For the cake:

²⁄₃ cup butter
6 ounces bittersweet chocolate, chopped
2 eggs
6 tablespoons sugar
2 tablespoons vegetable oil
1 teaspoon vanilla extract
²⁄₃ cup sifted all-purpose flour

For the filling:

4 1-ounce pieces bittersweet or
 white chocolate

PAN FOUR ¹⁄₂-CUP RAMEKINS, GENEROUSLY
GREASED AND SUGARED.

1 First, before preheating your oven, place a 9 x 13-inch baking pan on the lowest rack in the oven. Fill it with at least 1 inch of water. Position another rack above this pan in the middle of the oven. Now turn the oven on to preheat. The pan full of water will help keep the cakes moist.
2 Melt the butter and 6 ounces of bittersweet chocolate together in a heatproof bowl over simmering water, stirring to combine. Set aside.
3 In a medium bowl, combine the eggs, sugar, oil, and vanilla. Beat until the sugar is dissolved and the batter is thick and pale yellow. Gradually mix in the flour. Stir chocolate mixture into the batter until thoroughly combined.
4 Divide the batter equally among the ramekins and place them on a baking sheet. Bake at 350 degrees for 15 minutes.
5 Remove the cakes from the oven and place a 1-ounce piece of bittersweet or white chocolate into the middle of each cake. Press down with the tip of a knife to make sure the chocolate is completely submerged.
6 Return to the oven and bake for another 10 to 15 minutes, until a tester inserted in the edge of the cake comes out dry. (Don't insert the tester in the center or you will run into the melted chocolate). When the cakes are done, remove them from the oven. Let set 10 to 15 minutes. Run a knife around the edge of the ramekins and invert onto individual serving plates.

PRESENTATION Serve the cakes with a dollop of whipped cream or ice cream.

VARIATION
For the filling, use 2 ounces of bittersweet chocolate and 2 ounces of white chocolate. Cut into 1/2-ounce pieces and insert a piece of each kind of chocolate in each cake to get the best of both worlds.

one can find earlier references to it, and it's probable that housewives had been making the cake and exchanging their favorite recipes several years before that. Caroline King, a popular food writer of the 1920s and 30s, reminisces about growing up in Illinois in the mid-1880s, and describes Devil's Food Cake as being "all the rage" in bustling Chicago. The recipe is adapted from the one given in her book and yields a lighter-chocolate-colored cake than what is often called Devil's Food today.

1 1/4 cups all-purpose flour

1/2 teaspoon baking powder

1/2 teaspoon baking soda

1/4 cup unsalted butter, at room temperature

1 cup sugar

2 large eggs, separated

2 ounces unsweetened chocolate

1/2 teaspoon vanilla extract

1/2 cup sour cream

PAN 8-INCH ROUND PAN, GREASED AND FLOURED.

1 Measure the flour, baking powder, and baking soda into a bowl. Stir to combine and set aside.

2 In a separate bowl, cream the butter. Add the sugar gradually, creaming continuously until light and fluffy.

3 Lightly beat the egg yolks and combine with the butter–sugar mixture.

DEVIL'S FOOD CAKE

Similar to the dark chocolate cakes of Europe, Devil's Food Cake is an American invention. According to food historians, the exact origin of the name isn't known, but the leading theory is that this tempting treat was named in contrast to another popular cake of the era—the lighter, "purer" Angel Food. The first printed recipes appeared in cookbooks around the turn of the twentieth century. However,

4 Melt the chocolate in a heatproof bowl over simmering water. Add the melted chocolate and vanilla to the butter–sugar–egg yolk mixture.

5 Alternately add the flour mixture and the sour cream, beating well after each addition. The batter will be stiff, so be sure to scrape the sides of the bowl often.

6 Beat the egg whites to form stiff peaks and gently fold into the batter.

7 Pour the batter into prepared pan. Because this batter is stiff, use a spatula to level the top. Bake at 350 degrees for 30 to 35 minutes.

PRESENTATION I like this cake best with chocolate or vanilla frosting—try Basic Chocolate or Basic Vanilla, White Chocolate Buttercream, Buttery Chocolate Glaze, White Chocolate Meringue, Chocolate Meringue, or Chocolate Chip Cream Cheese Frostings (pages 96-100).

Polka Dot Devil's Food Cake
Before folding in the beaten egg whites, mix in 1 cup mini white chocolate chips.

Black Forest Devil's Food Cake
When the cake is cool, cut in half to make two layers. Spread Bing Cherry Filling (page 105) over the bottom half of the cake. Replace the top. Cover the top of the cake with whipped cream and garnish with grated chocolate or frost the cake with Chocolate Buttercream Frosting (page 98).

Raspberry Decadence Cake
Cut a Devil's Food Cake in half horizontally. Prepare one recipe each of Buttery Chocolate Glaze (page 98) and Raspberry Whipped Cream (page 95). Spread half of the glaze over the bottom half of the cake. Place in refrigerator 5 to 10 minutes until firmed. Spread the raspberry cream over the firmed glaze. Replace top half of cake and spread with remaining glaze. If cake is not to be served immediately, refrigerate until 10 to 15 minutes before serving.

Sacher Torte
Bake a Devil's Food Cake and once cooled, spread the top with a thin layer of a jam of your choice — apricot is traditional but raspberry or bing cherry is nice too. Then, frost the top and sides of the cake with Chocolate Ganache (page 97).

TIP Keep a paring or table knife handy when you bake. The back of the blade is perfect for leveling ingredients in measuring cups and spoons.

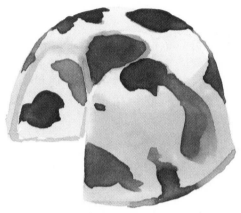

FUDGE MARBLE CAKE

Most people think there's only one kind of marble cake—the Fudge Marble listed here. In fact, back in the days when people always baked from scratch, there were a few types of marble. As late as the mid-1950s, cookbooks called this "Modern Marble" to distinguish it from its older cousin, Marble Spice (page 66).

1 3/4 cups sifted cake flour
2 teaspoons baking powder
1/2 teaspoon salt
1/2 cup unsalted butter, at room temperature
1 cup sugar
1/2 teaspoon vanilla
2 large eggs
1/2 cup plus 2 tablespoons milk
1 1/2 ounces semisweet chocolate

PAN 8-INCH ROUND OR SQUARE PAN, GREASED AND FLOURED.

1 Place the flour, baking powder, and salt in a bowl. Stir to combine and set aside.
2 Cream the butter until smooth. Add the sugar and vanilla and beat until light and fluffy.
3 Add the eggs one at a time, beating thoroughly after each addition.
4 Add half of dry ingredients and mix well. Add 1/4 cup of milk and mix well. Repeat with remaining dry ingredients and another 1/4 cup of milk.
5 Divide the batter in two bowls. Melt the chocolate in the remaining 2 tablespoons of milk, stirring to make a smooth, even mixture. Add the chocolate to half of the batter and mix thoroughly.
6 Drop the batter into the prepared pan 1 to 2 heaping tablespoons at a time, alternating light batter with chocolate. When all the batter is in the pan, swirl a knife through to enhance marbling. Rap the pan against the counter a few times to level batter. Bake at 350 degrees for 30 to 35 minutes.

PRESENTATION Chocolate is the perfect— and traditional—topping for this cake, be it Basic Chocolate or Chocolate Meringue (pages 96 and 100).

GERMAN CHOCOLATE CAKE

If you were around in the late 1950s, you probably still remember the stir caused by German Chocolate Cake. And you probably assumed this lovely concoction of not-quite-devil's-food layered with pecan-and-coconut-studded filling was Germany's most popular export. In fact, the cake owes its name to the brand of chocolate used in the original recipe, Baker's German's Chocolate. It was named for Sam German, the employee who had originally formulated it in 1852.

1 1/4 cups sifted cake flour

1/4 teaspoon salt

1/2 teaspoon baking soda

1/4 cup water

2 ounces Baker's German's sweet chocolate, chopped

1/2 cup unsalted butter, at room temperature

1 cup sugar

2 large eggs, separated

1/2 teaspoon vanilla extract

1/2 cup evaporated milk

1 Combine the sifted flour, salt, and baking soda and set aside.

2 Bring the water to a boil, take it off the heat, and stir in the chocolate to melt. Set aside.

3 Cream the butter. Add the sugar and continue to beat until light and fluffy. Add the egg yolks one at a time, beating well after each addition.

4 Beat in the melted chocolate and vanilla.

5 Add half of the flour mixture, then half of the evaporated milk, mixing well. Repeat with the remaining flour and evaporated milk.

6 Beat egg whites until stiff but not dry. Gently fold the egg whites into the chocolate mixture. Pour into prepared pan.

7 Bake at 350 degrees for 30 to 35 minutes.

PRESENTATION German Chocolate Cake wouldn't be complete without its trademark Coconut Pecan Frosting (page 103). You can use the entire recipe to frost the top or cut the cooled cake in half to make two layers and use half of the frosting as filling and the remaining half on the top of the cake.

FLOURLESS CHOCOLATE CAKE

Flourless chocolate cakes were the rage of the 1980s, appearing on restaurant dessert menus everywhere. Now, happily, they've become a classic. Whether you're a novice baker or a pro, this cake deserves a place in your lineup—it's elegant, easy, and needs no frosting, making it the perfect recipe to go to when you're in a pinch.

4 ounces bittersweet chocolate, chopped
$^1/_2$ cup unsalted butter, at room temperature
$^1/_2$ cup sugar
$^1/_4$ cup firmly packed brown sugar
3 large eggs
$^1/_2$ cup unsweetened cocoa powder

PAN 8-INCH ROUND PAN. PREPARE BY LINING THE BOTTOM WITH WAX PAPER, THEN LIGHTLY BUTTER BOTH THE PAPER AND THE SIDES OF THE PAN.

1 Melt the chocolate with the butter over simmering water, stirring continuously. When the mixture is completely smooth, transfer to a mixing bowl and whisk in the sugars.
2 Add the eggs one at a time, whisking well after each addition.
3 Sift the cocoa into the batter and mix just until combined.
4 Pour into the prepared pan and bake at 350 degrees for 25 to 35 minutes. This cake cannot be tested for doneness by the usual methods. Instead, look for a thin crust to form on the top, and jiggle the pan a bit to make sure the center has completely set.

PRESENTATION This cake needs no frosting, although some people like to beautify it with a thin coating of Chocolate Ganache (page 97). Personally, I prefer it with no frosting at all, just a generous cloud of not-too-sweet whipped cream.

WALDORF-ASTORIA RED VELVET CAKE

This cake was the sensation of the 1920s. Today the cake is reappearing as a popular retro treat. Individual heart-shaped molds can be used for a Valentine's Day treat.

1 cup plus 2 tablespoons sifted cake flour
1/2 teaspoon baking soda
1/2 teaspoon salt
2 teaspoons unsweetened cocoa powder
2/3 cup vegetable oil
3/4 cup sugar
1 large egg
1/2 teaspoon white vinegar
1/2 teaspoon vanilla extract
3 to 4 teaspoons red food coloring
1/2 cup buttermilk

PAN 8- OR 9-INCH HEART-SHAPED PAN, GREASED AND FLOURED.

1 Combine the flour, baking soda, salt, and cocoa in a bowl. Stir to combine and set aside.
2 Beat the oil and sugar together until well blended. Add the egg and blend well.
3 Mix in the vinegar, vanilla, and food coloring. The shade of this cake is a matter of individual taste, and varies from recipe to recipe. Add 2 teaspoons first, and the additional teaspoons only if desired. More food coloring will not make the cake redder, but a brighter, more cocoa-hued red. As you mix, remember that the color of the baked cake will be darker than the batter.
4 Add the flour mixture and buttermilk alternately, half of each at at time. Mix well but do not overbeat.
5 Pour into prepared pan and bake at 350 degrees for 25 to 30 minutes.

PRESENTATION For the most striking presentation, choose a white frosting for this cake — Basic Cream Cheese, Basic Buttercream, or White Chocolate Buttercream, for example (pages 98–100). Garnish with fresh raspberries or a little grated chocolate.

LOAF CAKES

Loaf cakes predate layered cakes by several centuries. Original loaf cakes, like loaves of bread, were often small and patted into shape, rather than poured into baking pans. The reason for this was that early cakes were stiff and heavy, hardly even what we think of as cakes today. Comprised largely of whole grains, what sweetness they possessed came from the addition of honey, nuts, and spices, not sugar and butter. Later, dried and candied fruits were added, along with sweeteners such as molasses and coarse brown sugar. These cakes, dense and heavy, were better suited to loaves than layers, and loaf cakes remained the standard well into the eighteenth and nineteenth centuries. In fact, before white flour and white sugar were widely available, these were common fare for weddings cakes—a tradition that can still be seen in regions where the groom's cake is dark, loaf-style fruitcake.

Today's loaf cakes have moved far beyond fruitcake. Some, like pound cake, are too rich and heavy to make good layer cakes while others are valued because they are simple, delicious cakes that slice easily and can be served without frosting.

MARBLE
POUND CAKE

The best of both worlds, and not to be missed!

1 ounce semisweet chocolate

1 1/2 cups sifted all-purpose flour

1/2 teaspoon baking soda

1/4 teaspoon salt

1/2 cup unsalted butter, at room temperature

1 1/4 cups sugar

1/2 teaspoon vanilla extract

3 large eggs

1/2 cup sour cream

PAN 9 X 5-INCH OR 8 1/4 X 4 1/4-INCH LOAF PAN, GREASED AND FLOURED.

1 Melt the chocolate in a heatproof bowl over simmering water. Set the bowl in a pan of very warm water to keep chocolate slightly warm.

2 Sift the flour, baking soda, and salt into a bowl and set aside.

3 In a mixing bowl, cream the butter, sugar and vanilla together. Add the eggs one at a time and beat until light and fluffy.

4 Add half of the flour mixture, then half of the sour cream, beating until combined after each addition. Repeat with remaining flour mixture and sour cream.

5 Pour two-thirds of the batter into prepared pan.

6 Add the melted chocolate to remaining batter and mix thoroughly to combine. Drop the chocolate mixture by spoonfuls into the pan. Using a narrow spatula, make a zigzag pattern through the batter to create a marbled effect. Make sure your spatula reaches all the way to the bottom of the pan so that the chocolate batter is evenly distributed from top to bottom.

7 Bake at 350 degrees for 40 to 50 minutes.

PRESENTATION Serve plain or with a small scoop of ice cream.

TIP Since this batter is thick, you can help things along by scooping a spoonful of yellow batter out wherever you want to put in chocolate. If you are using a metal spatula or knife, warm it under hot water.

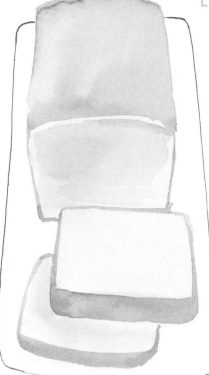

POUND CAKE

References to pound cake date back to the 1740s, and first appeared in England. As the name implies, the cake originally called for a pound each of its four basic ingredients: butter, flour, sugar, and eggs. This must have been a tremendous memory aid back in the days when few recipes were written down, and those that were often couldn't be read by the cooks who made them.

Everyone should know how to make good pound cake, as it is the most versatile of treats—delicious on its own, made elegant with fresh fruit and whipped cream, or reincarnated as an ethereal trifle. I particularly like this recipe because it makes two little loaves, one for immediate gratification and the other to freeze.

1 $1/3$ cups all-purpose flour
$1/4$ teaspoon baking powder, slightly rounded
Pinch of salt
$1/4$ teaspoon vanilla extract
$1/3$ cup milk
$2/3$ cup unsalted butter, at room temperature
1 cup sugar
2 large eggs
PAN TWO 5 $3/4$ X 3 $1/4$ -INCH LOAF PANS OR ONE STANDARD 9 X 5-INCH OR 8 $1/4$ X 4 $1/4$-INCH LOAF PAN, GREASED AND FLOURED.

1 Measure the flour, baking powder, and salt into a bowl. Stir to combine and set aside.
2 Add the vanilla to the milk and set aside.
3 Cream the butter until very light. Add the sugar gradually, beating continuously.
4 Add the eggs one at a time, mixing just until completely blended.
5 Add one-third of the dry ingredients to the butter-egg mixture, then half the milk, beating after each addition just until combined. Repeat with the next third of dry ingredients, the rest of the milk, and the remainder of the

dry ingredients, beating after each.

6 Pour into prepared pans and bake at 325 degrees, about 35 minutes for small loaves, 45 to 55 minutes for larger loaf. Don't be alarmed if your golden brown crust splits to reveal a strip of yellow cake—this is desirable in pound cake.

PRESENTATION Pound cake needs no frosting. In fact, one of the delights of good pound cake is its golden brown crust. Adding even a dusting of powdered sugar would dampen the crust's slight crispness. Instead, serve with fresh or frozen fruit, or add a dollop of one of the flavored whipped creams found on pages 94-95.

TIP If you are adapting your own favorite recipes for small cakes, remember one third is not midway between a quarter and a half. A quarter cup is four tablespoons, and a half cup is eight, but a third of a cup is five and a third tablespoons—one and a third tablespoons more than a quarter cup, but two and two thirds less than a half cup.

Coconut Pound Cake

Add $3/4$ cup shredded coconut to the finished batter.

Candied Ginger Pound Cake

Coarsely chop $1/2$ cup candied ginger and fold into batter.

Lemon Pound Cake

Mix 1 tablespoon of grated lemon zest into batter. This variation is particularly delicious with fresh blueberries.

Raspberry Pound Cake

Place half of the batter in pan and cover with fresh raspberries, about $1/2$ cup for a small loaf, or 1 cup for a large loaf. Top with remaining batter. Frozen raspberries, thawed and drained, can also be used.

Tipsy Cake

Although this is really just an individual form of Trifle (page 81), I include it here because it is best made with slices of leftover, very stale pound cake. First, dip the slices in sweet sherry or sweet dessert wine. Line the sides of wineglasses with the cake. Place a heaping spoonful of finely chopped almonds or pecans in the bottom of each glass, then layer with a spoonful of jam or finely chopped dates or raisins. Fill the glass almost to the top with Vanilla Custard (page 105), and top off with whipped cream.

TIP To make two completely different cakes in one baking session, measure half of batter (about $1 1/2$ cups) and set aside. Prepare each half of batter with half of the addition amounts suggested above and bake in $5 3/4$ x $3 1/4$-inch loaf pans.

CHOCOLATE POUND CAKE

1 ½ to 2 ounces semisweet chocolate
1 cup plus 6 tablespoons all-purpose flour
½ teaspoon cream of tartar
¼ teaspoon baking soda
¾ teaspoon salt
½ cup unsalted butter, at room temperature
¾ cup plus 2 tablespoons sugar
⅓ cup milk
½ teaspoon vanilla extract
2 large eggs
PAN 9 X 5-INCH OR 8 ¼ X 4 ¼ -INCH LOAF PAN, GREASED AND FLOURED.

1 Melt the chocolate in a heatproof bowl over simmering water. Set bowl in a pan of very warm water to keep chocolate slightly warm.
2 Measure the flour, cream of tartar, baking soda, and salt into bowl. Stir to combine and set aside.

3 Cream the butter until light. Add the sugar gradually, beating continuously. Mix in the flour mixture. Add the milk and vanilla and beat 2 minutes.
4 Add the eggs and chocolate and beat 1 minute.
5 Pour into prepared pan and bake at 350 degrees for 40 to 50 minutes.

PRESENTATION   Although this cake needs no frosting, you might want to drizzle Powdered Sugar Glaze (page 101) over the top. This cake is especially delicious with fresh raspberries or cherries.

TIP   The longer the baking time, the more impact the eccentricities of individual ovens can have. I recommend checking your pound cake after 40 minutes of baking, or even earlier if your oven tends to run hot. When your cake is done, jot down the time required in the margin.

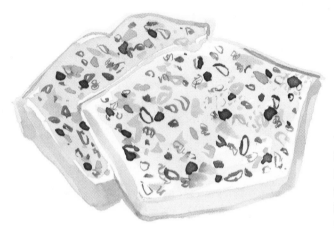

BUTTER PECAN LOAF

A particular treat on an autumn day.

1 1/3 cups all-purpose flour

2 teaspoons baking powder

1/2 teaspoon salt

1/3 cup unsalted butter,
   at room temperature

1/2 cup sugar

1/4 cup firmly packed brown sugar

1/2 teaspoon vanilla extract

1 large egg

2/3 cup milk

1/2 cup pecans, broken into pieces

PAN 9 X 5-INCH OR 8 1/4 X 4 1/4-INCH LOAF
PAN, GREASED AND FLOURED.

1 Measure the flour, baking powder, and salt into a bowl. Stir to combine and set aside.
2 Cream the butter until light, then add the sugars and vanilla. Add the egg and beat by hand until light and fluffy.
3 Mix in the dry ingredients, then the milk, and beat for 2 minutes. Fold in the pecans.
4 Pour into the prepared pan and bake at 350 degrees for 40 to 50 minutes.

PRESENTATION Serve plain, or when cool frost with Butter Pecan Icing or with Secret Ingredient Pecan Frosting (page 103).

FRUITCAKE

The oldest of loaf cakes, fruitcake became popular when sugar from the New World flooded the European market. For the first time, sugar became cheap enough to use in quantity, making it possible to preserve fruits both exotic and domestic. Voilà—the fruitcake, with its mélange of candied fruits and sweet batter. Today, fruitcake has fallen far from its glory days. But each December when I sit down to read Truman Capote's *A Christmas Memory*, a piece of dense, sticky fruitcake is just what I want to keep me company.

$1/2$ cup chopped pecans
$1/3$ cup chopped candied fruit
    (cherries, pineapple, citron, etc.)
$1/3$ cup chopped dried apricots
$1/3$ cup golden raisins
$1/2$ cup all-purpose flour
$1/4$ cup unsalted butter, at room temperature
$1/4$ cup firmly packed brown sugar
1 large egg
2 tablespoons orange juice
2 tablespoons honey
1 tablespoon milk
Scant $1/4$ teaspoon baking powder
$1/2$ teaspoon ground cinnamon
Pinch of ground nutmeg
Pinch of salt

PAN TWO 5 $3/4$ X 3 $1/4$ -INCH LOAF PANS. PREPARE PANS BY LINING THE BOTTOM OF EACH PAN WITH WAX PAPER, THEN GREASING AND FLOURING THE PAPER AND THE SIDES OF EACH PAN.

1 Toss the nuts, candied fruit, apricots, and raisins in a bowl with $1/4$ cup of the flour. Set aside.
2 Cream the butter and sugar together. Add the egg and beat well.
3 Add the orange juice, honey, and milk. Don't be alarmed if the mixture appears curdled.
4 Add the remaining flour, baking powder, cinnamon, nutmeg, and salt and mix well.
5 Mix in the fruit mixture, stirring well.
6 Spread in pans and bake at 300 degrees for 50 to 60 minutes.

PRESENTATION Cut cooled cake in $1/2$-inch slices and serve. Get in the holiday spirit — garnish plate with mint leaves and candied cherries to resemble holly.

POPPY SEED LOAF

Research into the origins of this wonderfully soft and delicate loaf inevitably lead back to Hungary, and the presence of sour cream reinforces that idea. Before you try the lemon variation below, try the basic version, whose subtle taste can become addictive.

1/4 cup unsalted butter, at room temperature

3/4 cup sugar

2 large eggs, separated

1/2 cup sour cream

1/2 teaspoon baking soda

1 cup all-purpose flour

1 teaspoon vanilla extract

1/4 cup poppy seeds

PAN 9 X 5-INCH OR 8 1/4 X 4 1/4 -INCH LOAF PAN, GREASED.

1 Cream the butter, sugar, and egg yolks until light and fluffy.

2 Mix in the sour cream and baking soda until blended.

3 Add the flour, vanilla, and poppy seeds.

4 Beat the eggs whites until stiff and fold into the batter.

5 Bake at 350 degrees 45 to 55 minutes.

PRESENTATION This cake needs no frosting, and is delicious on its own or with sliced fresh fruit – blueberries and sliced fresh strawberries are particularly delicious.

Lemon Poppy Seed Loaf

Make as a Poppy Seed Loaf, but before you add the flour, add 2 tablespoons of lemon juice and 1 to 2 teaspoons grated lemon zest. A slice of this is particularly good with a small scoop of lemon sherbet, or you can frost the cake with Lemon Glaze, page 101.

FRUIT AND NUT CAKES

My mother once told me about going into a grocery store after the war and seeing a surprising new food item: cake mixes. No doubt their 1947 debut seemed a miracle, especially to young wives like my mother, for whom the privations of the Depression had been followed by the shortages of the war. With only eggs, oil, and water to add, and one of the new electric mixers to do the work, thousands of women must have released a vast collective sigh of appreciation—along with their families, who could now look forward to having cake far more often than before.

But all this upside had one big downside: loss of variety. While cookbooks boasted hundreds of recipes and dozens of types of cakes, mass production accommodated no such diversity, and choices were soon pared down to a handful. One of the best reasons to learn to bake from scratch is to rediscover these lost classics.

LEMON
PUDDING CAKE

Although today the word "pudding" conjures up a custard-like dessert, it wasn't always so. Bread pudding, Indian pudding, and cottage pudding relied on grains for body, and were served with a variety of flavored sauces. Eventually, this type of pudding was made with the sauce inside, and pudding cake was born. Particularly popular in the 1950s and 1960s, pudding cake resurfaced under a variety of names in the 1990s, including "molten" and "lava." So whether you want to call this Lemon Pudding Cake or Lemon Vesuvius, enjoy its perfect blend of sharp taste and warm comfort.

1/4 cup sifted all-purpose flour

3/4 cup sugar

1/4 teaspoon salt

2 large eggs, separated

1 1/2 teaspoons unsalted butter,
   at room temperature

3 tablespoons lemon juice

1/2 teaspoon grated lemon zest

3/4 cup milk

PAN FOUR INDIVIDUAL OVENPROOF RAMEKINS, GREASED AND FLOURED.

NOTE This recipe can be doubled and made in an 8-inch square pan.

1 Stir the flour, sugar, and salt to combine and set aside.
2 In a mixing bowl, beat the egg yolks, butter, lemon juice, and zest until thick.
3 Add the dry ingredients and milk alternately to egg–lemon mixture, beating well after each addition.
4 In a separate bowl, beat the egg whites until stiff. Fold gently into batter.
5 Divide the batter among the four ramekins. Set the ramekins in a pan with about an inch of water, place the pan in the oven, and bake at 350 degrees for approximately 30 minutes.

PRESENTATION Serve warm, dusted with a little powdered sugar if you wish.

FRESH
APPLE CAKE

Apples were one of the first fruits used in cakes, as their abundance and natural sweetness made them a staple commodity. Everyone could afford apples, and the fact that they could be easily dried made them one of the few fruits available in the harsh winter months. The earliest cakes involved sliced apples brushed with honey and wrapped in pastry, while stack cakes (thin layers of cake sandwiched with fruit) frequently used dried apples as a filling ingredient. Cake recipes using applesauce were popular in the era when every housewife had jar upon jar of home-canned applesauce. However, now that fresh apples are available year round, I like this recipe better. It's a perfect cake for a picnic or an informal Saturday night supper.

For the cake:

1 small to medium Granny Smith apple

1 ½ cups sifted all-purpose flour

½ teaspoon salt

1 ¾ teaspoons baking powder

½ cup sugar

¼ teaspoon ground allspice

¼ teaspoon ground nutmeg

⅓ cup unsalted butter, at room temperature

1 large egg

¼ cup milk

For the topping:

¼ cup unsalted butter, melted

¾ teaspoon ground cinnamon,
   mixed with 2 tablespoons sugar

PAN 8-INCH ROUND OR SQUARE PAN,
GREASED AND FLOURED.

Make the cake:

1 Peel, core, and coarsely grate the apple
to make ½ to ⅔ cup. Set aside.

2 In a mixing bowl, combine the flour, salt,
baking powder, ½ sugar, allspice, and nutmeg.

3 Cut the butter into the flour mixture,
using a fork or pastry blender until pieces are
the size of a pea. (This can also be done by
pulsing in a food processor.) The mixture will
be dry and crumbly.

4 In another bowl, beat the egg lightly
with a fork. Add the milk and grated apple.
Add to the flour–butter mixture. Mix just until
thoroughly combined.

5 Pour into prepared pan and bake at 350
degrees for 23 to 28 minutes.

Make the topping:

1 While cake is baking, melt the butter and
set aside. Combine the cinnamon and sugar
and set aside.

2 When the cake is finished and still warm
(but not hot), brush top with melted butter.
Sprinkle with the cinnamon–sugar mixture.

ORANGE CAKE

I tried adapting several recipes for an orange cake and was disappointed every time. One little gem even turned itself into a large donut, with an air hole in the middle. I finally came up with this idea, which yielded delectable results. The moistness of this cake may cause it to flatten slightly in the center, but don't despair—the flavor is more than adequate compensation.

1 medium orange
1 cup sifted cake flour
1 1/2 teaspoons baking powder
1/2 cup unsalted butter, at room temperature
3/4 cup sugar
2 large eggs, separated
Pinch of salt

PAN 8-INCH ROUND PAN, LIGHTLY GREASED.

1 Place the whole, unpeeled orange in a pot of boiling water and boil for 10 minutes. Remove and set aside until cool enough to handle.

2 When the orange is cool, grate the skin with a grater. The softened orange grates more easily than you're used to, so be careful not to grate into the pith. Set grated peel aside.

3 Peel off and discard the remaining peel. Separate the orange into sections and remove the membrane. Break the sections into a bowl and remove all seeds. Transfer the orange flesh to a food processor and pulse to make a pulp. (If you don't have a food processor, finely mince the orange, retaining the juice as well as the pulp.) Set the orange aside.

4 Place the sifted flour and baking powder in a bowl. Stir to combine and set aside.

5 In a mixing bowl, cream the butter. Add the sugar and grated orange zest, creaming until light and fluffy.

6 Add the egg yolks one at a time, beating after each addition.

7 Add the dry ingredients alternately with the orange pulp, one-half of each at a time.

8 In another bowl, beat the egg whites until soft peaks form. Add the salt and beat until stiff.

9 Gently fold the egg whites into the batter. Spoon into the prepared pan and spread evenly. Bake at 350 degrees for about 35 minutes.

PRESENTATION The intense orange flavor should not be diluted. Frost this cake with the Orange Buttercream on page 99 or Orange Glaze on page 101.

BLACKBERRY JAM CAKE

Jam cake was a favorite on the American frontier, where every larder was sure to have an abundance of preserves put up by enterprising women. It's still a good cake to make, even with store-bought jam.

1 ½ cups all-purpose flour
½ teaspoon baking soda
1 teaspoon ground allspice
1 teaspoon ground cloves
1 teaspoon ground cinnamon
1 teaspoon ground nutmeg
½ cup unsalted butter, at room temperature
1 cup sugar
3 large eggs
½ cup buttermilk
½ cup blackberry jam

PAN 8-INCH ROUND OR SQUARE PAN, GREASED AND FLOURED.

1 Sift the flour, baking soda, allspice, cloves, cinnamon, and nutmeg together and set aside.
2 Cream the butter and sugar until light and fluffy. Add the eggs one at a time, beating well after each addition.
3 Add the dry ingredients alternately with the buttermilk, about one-third of each at a time, mixing well after each addition.
4 Add the jam and mix thoroughly.
5 Turn into a prepared pan and bake at 350 degrees for 25 to 30 minutes.

PRESENTATION Traditionally, this cake is served with the Caramel Icing (page 104). It is also good plain, or served with a dollop of whipped cream dusted with a sprinkling of nutmeg.

NOTE This cake can be made with almost any type of jam, such as berry, cherry, citrus, and black currant.

Cherry Nut Jam Cake

Use cherry or sour cherry preserves instead of blackberry and mix ½ cup chopped pecans into the finished batter before pouring into the prepared pan.

Blueberry Lemon Jam Cake

Replace the blackberry jam with blueberry and omit the cloves. Mix 1 teaspoon grated lemon zest into the batter before pouring into the prepared pan.

Orange Marmalade Cake

Replace blackberry jam with orange marmalade, and mix 1 teaspoon grated orange zest into batter before pouring into prepared pan.

1 Sift the flour, baking powder, baking soda, and salt into a bowl and stir to combine. Set aside.

2 Cream the butter until light. Add the sugar, creaming continuously until fluffy. Add the egg and beat thoroughly. Mix in the vanilla.

3 Stir the buttermilk into the mashed banana.

4 Alternately add the dry ingredients and banana mixture to the butter–sugar mixture, about one-third of each at a time. Beat thoroughly after each addition.

5 Pour into the prepared pan and bake at 350 degrees for 25 to 30 minutes.

BANANA CAKE

This moist, dense, and firm banana cake keeps well and, uniced, is perfect for picnics. With icing, it's a slice of heaven.

1 cup plus 2 tablespoons sifted cake flour

1 1/4 teaspoons baking powder

1/4 teaspoon baking soda

1/4 teaspoon salt

1/4 cup unsalted butter, at room temperature

1/2 cup sugar

1 large egg

1/2 teaspoon vanilla extract

2 tablespoons buttermilk

1/2 cup mashed overripe banana

PAN 8- OR 9-INCH ROUND PAN, GREASED AND FLOURED.

PRESENTATION Older recipes call this "Gold Nugget Cake," and called for spreading it with whipped cream and arranging nuggets of sliced bananas over the top. Equally delicious is finishing with Basic Cream Cheese Frosting (page 100), and post-modernists might want to indulge in a chocolate icing or glaze, Caramel Icing, or the Peanut Butter Frosting (page 104).

NOTE The more overripe your bananas are, the more flavor your cake will have. Personally, I won't consider any banana whose skin hasn't turned dark brown or black and begun to shrivel. To speed the ripening of bananas, place them in a paper bag, twist the top closed, and put in a dark cupboard for a few days.

GRAPEFRUIT CAKE

This cake was popularized by Hollywood's Brown Derby Restaurant, and was reputedly a favorite of actress Joanne Woodward, who ordered it whenever she dined there. If it can make the rest of us as lovely and glowing as the actress, we want second helpings.

1 cup sifted cake flour

$1/2$ cup sugar

1 teaspoon baking powder

$1/4$ teaspoon salt

2 large eggs, separated

2 tablespoons water

2 tablespoons plus 2 teaspoons grapefruit juice

2 tablespoons plus 2 teaspoons oil

PAN 8-INCH ROUND PAN, GREASED AND FLOURED.

1 Place the sifted flour, sugar, baking powder, and salt in a mixing bowl and stir to combine. Set aside.

2 Whisk the egg yolks. Stir in the water, grapefruit juice, and oil.

3 In another bowl, beat the egg whites until stiff but not dry.

4 Pour the egg yolk mixture into the flour mixture. Beat on low until combined, then beat at medium speed for 2 minutes.

5 Fold the beaten egg whites into the cake batter and pour into the prepared pan.

6 Bake at 350 degrees for 25 to 30 minutes.

7 When completely cool, frost with Grapefruit Frosting, page 101. You can either use all the frosting on top of the cake, letting it drift lavishly over the sides, or you can cut the cake in half crosswise and use half between the layers.

PRESENTATION Many recipes call for arranging canned grapefruit segments on top of the cake or between the layers. I think this makes for a soggy cake and unattractive leftovers. Instead, garnish the top of the cake with a little grated orange zest and serve a few segments of fresh pink grapefruit on the side.

PINEAPPLE UPSIDE-DOWN CAKE

Pineapple upside-down cake is a descendant of skillet cake—cakes made in a cast-iron skillet, with a layer of fruit on the bottom that became the topping when the finished cake was inverted. Although the inversion method had been practiced since the Middle Ages, "Upside-down" did not appear as a cake name until the mid-1800s, and pineapple only became an ingredient after James Dole began canning it in 1903. It isn't known exactly when or who developed the first recipe, but when Dole sponsored a recipe contest in 1925, more that 2,500 recipes for upside-down cake were submitted. Seeing a popular new use for their product, Dole built an add campaign around the cake, and soon began printing the recipe on the back of the label.

For pineapple topping:

1 (20-ounce) can pineapple-rings, chunks, or crushed

$1/4$ cup unsalted butter

$2/3$ cup packed brown sugar

Maraschino cherries or pecan halves (optional)

For the cake:

$1 1/2$ cups all-purpose flour

$1 1/2$ teaspoons baking powder

$1/2$ teaspoon salt

$1/2$ cup unsalted butter, at room temperature

$2/3$ cup sugar

2 large eggs

$1/2$ teaspoon vanilla extract

$3/4$ cup milk

PAN 8-INCH SQUARE PAN, PREPARED BY CUTTING A PIECE OF WAX PAPER TO FIT THE BOTTOM, THEN BUTTERING THE PAPER AND THE SIDES OF THE PAN.

Make pineapple topping:

1 Drain the pineapple well and set aside. Juice can be discarded or reserved for other use.

2 In a saucepan, melt the butter over low heat. Remove from heat and stir in brown sugar. Spread evenly over the bottom of the wax paper-lined pan.

3 Arrange the pineapple over butter–brown sugar mixture. If you wish, add a few maraschino cherries and/or pecan halves as well.

Make the cake:

1 Place the flour, baking powder, and salt in a bowl. Stir to combine and set aside.
2 In a mixing bowl, cream the butter. Add the sugar, and cream until light and fluffy.
3 Add the eggs one at a time, beating well after each addition. Mix in the vanilla.
4 Add one-third of the dry ingredients and half of the milk, beating well after each addition. Repeat, and finish by adding remaining dry ingredients.
5 Spread the batter over the pineapple topping in the pan. Bake at 350 degrees for 35 to 45 minutes.
6 When the cake is done, let set 5 to 10 minutes, then loosen by running a knife around the edge. Invert onto serving plate. Let sit 15 minutes, then remove the pan and carefully peel away the waxed paper.

PRESENTATION Serve warm with whipped cream.

Apple Upside-Down Cake

Replace the pineapple with sliced fresh peeled apples, about 1 1/2 to 2 cups. Stir 1 teaspoon ground cinnamon into the saucepan as you make the butter-brown sugar topping.

Berry Upside-Down Cake

Replace the pineapple with 1 1/2 cups fresh blueberries, raspberries, blackberries, or a combination of all three.

Caramel Nut Upside-Down Cake

Instead of fruit, scatter 2/3 cup pecans over the butter-brown sugar mixture in the bottom of the pan.

Hawaiian Upside-Down Cake

Before arranging the pineapple, scatter 1/2 cup shredded coconut and 1/2 cup chopped macadamia nuts over butter-brown sugar mixture.

Peach Upside-Down Cake

Replace the pineapple with slices of canned or fresh, peeled peaches or a combination of peaches and fresh or frozen raspberries.

Pear Upside-Down Cake

Replace the pineapple with canned or fresh, peeled pear slices. Before topping with the cake batter, sprinkle the pears lightly with ground cinnamon, allspice, and a bit of ginger.

PIONEER RAISIN SPICE CAKE

This recipe came from my great-grandmother's family, and was made in Iowa during the Civil War. It makes a thick, hearty cake that freezes well and can double as a coffee cake.

2 cups all-purpose flour

1 teaspoon baking powder

1 teaspoon baking soda

1 teaspoon ground cinnamon

1 teaspoon ground cloves

$\frac{1}{2}$ teaspoon ground nutmeg

1 $\frac{1}{2}$ cups raisins

$\frac{1}{2}$ cup unsalted butter, at room temperature

1 cup sugar

$\frac{1}{2}$ cup packed brown sugar

2 large eggs

1 cup cold liquid coffee

PAN 8 - OR 9 - INCH SQUARE PAN, GREASED AND FLOURED.

1 Measure the flour, baking powder, baking soda, cinnamon, cloves, and nutmeg into a bowl. Stir to combine and set aside.

2 In a saucepan, cover the raisins with water and bring to boil. Boil for 2 minutes, drain well, and set aside.

3 In a mixing bowl, cream the butter until light. Add the sugars and beat until light and fluffy. Add the eggs one at a time, beating well after each addition.

4 Add one-third of the dry ingredients, then half of coffee, mixing well after each addition. Repeat, then end with the remaining dry ingredients.

5 Stir in the raisins.

6 Bake at 350 degrees for approximately 35 minutes.

PRESENTATION This cake is perfect without frosting. Serve plain or dust with a little powdered sugar.

OATMEAL CAKE

This cake did not become popular until after World War II. The frosting of choice—Penuche—is also representative of the 1950s, when Americans reached out to embrace "exotic" foreign foods.

$^3/_4$ cup boiling water

$^1/_2$ cup oatmeal (not quick or instant)

$^1/_4$ cup unsalted butter, at room temperature

$^1/_2$ cup packed brown sugar

$^1/_2$ cup sugar

1 large egg

$^3/_4$ cup sifted all-purpose flour

$^1/_2$ teaspoon baking soda

$^1/_2$ teaspoon ground cinnamon

$^1/_2$ teaspoon ground allspice

$^1/_4$ teaspoon salt

PAN 8-INCH ROUND OR SQUARE PAN, GREASED AND FLOURED.

1 Pour the boiling water over the oatmeal. Let stand 20 minutes.

2 Cream the butter. Add the sugars and egg and beat until light and fluffy.

3 Add the flour, baking soda, cinnamon, allspice, and salt and mix well.

4 Add the oatmeal and stir until well mixed.

5 Pour into prepared pan and bake at 350 degrees for 20 to 25 minutes.

PRESENTATION This cake is most often served with Penuche Frosting (page 104), although cream cheese frostings and powdered sugar glazes are also delicious. It is good unfrosted or with a dusting of powdered sugar, and makes a good lunchbox or picnic cake.

PUMPKIN CAKE

Like carrot cake, pumpkin cake came to sudden popularity in the 1970s. I have made this cake hundreds of times and never had a failure. In a 6-inch springform pan it makes a high-domed cake that is tender, delicious, and perfect for Halloween, Thanksgiving, or an autumn birthday.

½ cup all-purpose flour
½ teaspoon baking powder
¼ teaspoon baking soda
1 teaspoon ground cinnamon
½ teaspoon ground allspice
¼ teaspoon ground nutmeg
⅛ teaspoon salt
1 large egg
½ cup sugar
¼ cup vegetable oil
5 tablespoons canned pumpkin
     (not pumpkin pie filling)

PAN 6-INCH SPRINGFORM OR OTHER 6-INCH ROUND PAN, GREASED AND FLOURED.

1 Measure the flour, baking powder, baking soda, cinnamon, allspice, nutmeg, and salt into bowl. Stir to combine and set aside.
2 In a mixing bowl, beat the egg lightly. Add the sugar and oil and mix well, until slightly frothy and well combined.
3 Mix the pumpkin into the egg mixture.
4 Add the dry ingredients to the egg-pumpkin mixture and beat, about 1 minute, until well combined.
5 Pour into prepared pan and bake at 350 degrees for approximately 30 minutes.

PRESENTATION Cream Cheese Frosting (page 100) is a perfect topping for this cake, garnished with a light sprinkling of nutmeg. If you don't wish to have frosting, it is also good dusted with powdered sugar, or with a scoop of vanilla or butter pecan ice cream.

TIP Wondering what to do with the leftover pumpkin? There are many tasty things you can do with leftover pumpkin. Try your hand at the Individual Upside-Down Pumpkin Cheesecakes on page 87, or make pumpkin soup, pumpkin bread, a small pumpkin pie, or a pumpkin smoothie.

GINGERBREAD

Gingerbread originated in western Europe almost a millennium ago, when returning crusaders introduced Europe to the exotic spices of the Holy Land. According to one theory, monasteries produced the first version of this food, first mixing spices with honey and spreading it on bread, then incorporating the honey and spices into the dough itself. The treat soon began appearing as a festival food at country fairs and at holiday times. Bakers across northern Europe began creating their own specialized versions. Some continued to make it as a flat, crisp cookie; others molded the stiff dough into the shape of people or animals; and still others added liquid to the batter to create a soft, spice-filled cake. In France and England, gingerbread bakers belonged to their own guilds, and held a monopoly on the right to make and sell the confection. Gingerbread as we know it today is a blend of the Old World and the New. When West Indies molasses became a popular eighteenth-century export, bakers in Europe as well as North America seized on it as a popular, inexpensive replacement for honey. Soon it was found that the dark, sticky sweetener was a perfect complement to ginger's sharpness.

2 cups sifted cake flour
2 teaspoons baking powder
$1/4$ teaspoon baking soda

1 tablespoon ground ginger
2 teaspoons ground allspice
$1/2$ teaspoon salt
$1/3$ cup unsalted butter, at room temperature
$1/4$ cup packed brown sugar
1 large egg
$2/3$ cup dark molasses
$3/4$ cup buttermilk
PAN 8- OR 9-INCH SQUARE PAN, GREASED.

1 Combine the sifted flour, baking powder, baking soda, ginger, allspice, and salt in a bowl. Stir to combine and set aside.
2 Cream the butter. Gradually add the sugar, creaming until light and fluffy.
3 Beat in the egg, then the molasses.
4 Add one-quarter flour–spice mixture, then one-third of the milk, beating until smooth after each addition. Repeat twice, ending with the last quarter of the flour–spice mixture.
5 Pour the batter into the prepared pan and smooth the top with a spatula to make it level.
6 Bake at 350 degrees for 45 to 50 minutes.

PRESENTATION Gingerbread is never frosted. In America, the traditional way to serve it is with a dollop of whipped cream. However, I prefer the way it is traditionally eaten in Britain: spread with cold, unsalted butter.

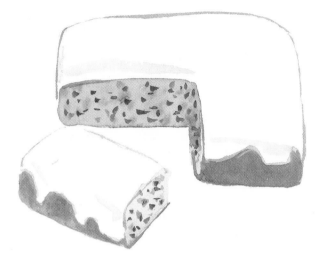

CARROT CAKE

Though it was the rave spice cake of the 1970s, carrot cake isn't new at all. According to Jean Anderson's excellent detective work in *The American Century Cookbook*, George Washington once dined on carrot cake, and examples of the recipe appeared in American cookbooks as early as 1929. Many of these, however, used a puree of cooked carrots, and the new twist of the whole foods era was to use raw carrots in the mix.

1 $^1/_4$ cups all-purpose flour
$^3/_4$ teaspoon baking powder
$^1/_2$ teaspoon baking soda
$^1/_4$ teaspoon salt
1 teaspoon ground cinnamon

$^1/_4$ teaspoon ground allspice
2 large eggs
$^1/_2$ cup sugar
$^1/_2$ cup packed brown sugar
$^3/_4$ cup vegetable oil
1 $^1/_2$ cups grated carrots (about 3 medium peeled carrots, or $^1/_2$ pound)
PAN 8-INCH ROUND OR SQUARE PAN, GREASED AND FLOURED.

1 Measure the flour, baking powder and soda, salt, cinnamon, and allspice into a bowl. Stir to combine and set aside.
2 In a mixing bowl, beat the eggs with the sugars until frothy.
3 Add the oil in a steady stream while continuing to beat.
4 Stir in the grated carrots.
5 Add the dry ingredients, and mix just until thoroughly combined.
6 Pour into the prepared pan and bake at 350 degrees for 25 to 30 minutes.

PRESENTATION Basic Cream Cheese Frosting (page 100) is a must for this cake, either plain or flavored with cardamom or lemon. If you want to embellish your cake, use colored frosting to pipe on decorative carrots.

TIP If you're out of allspice but have cloves (or vice versa), substitute half as much cloves for the allspice.

Raisin Walnut Carrot Cake

In a saucepan, cover $1/2$ cup raisins with water and bring to boil. Remove from the heat. Let stand a few minutes, then drain well. Stir the drained raisins into the finished batter along with $1/2$ cup chopped walnuts. Pour into the pan and bake.

Tropical Carrot Cake

Drain and dice enough canned pineapple to make $1/2$ cup. (Rings or chunks you dice yourself work better than crushed pineapple, which can make the cake soggy.) Add to the batter with the carrots, along with $1/2$ cup shredded coconut. Bake the cake as described in the basic recipe.

WALNUT CAKE

This is an Americanized version of the traditional Eastern European dessert, right down to its apple topping.

1 cup plus 3 tablespoons all-purpose flour
$3/4$ teaspoon baking soda
$1/3$ cup unsalted butter, at room temperature

$1/3$ cup sugar
$1/3$ cup packed brown sugar
1 large egg
$1/2$ cup buttermilk
$1/2$ teaspoon vanilla extract
$1/2$ cup coarsely ground walnuts
PAN 8-INCH ROUND PAN, GREASED AND FLOURED.

1 Measure the flour and baking soda into a bowl. Stir to combine and set aside.
2 In a mixing bowl, lightly cream the butter. Add the sugars, creaming continuously until light and fluffy. Add the egg and beat well.
3 Add half of the dry ingredients, then half of the buttermilk and all of the vanilla, stirring just until combined after each addition. Repeat with remaining ingredients.
4 Fold in the walnuts. Spread in the prepared pan and bake at 350 degrees for 23 to 28 minutes.

PRESENTATION Adorn each slice of cake with a spoonful of Spiced Apple Topping (page 106) and a generous dollop of Whipped Cream (page 93) sprinkled with cinnamon or nutmeg. This cake can also be finished with Basic or Coffee Buttercream Frosting (pages 98–99).

COFFEE-FLAVORED SPONGE CAKE

Light and not-too-heavy, this is perfect for an afternoon snack.

1 tablespoon light molasses

1 teaspoon instant coffee powder

$3/4$ cup plus 1 tablespoon all-purpose flour

$1/2$ teaspoon baking powder

Pinch of salt

$1/2$ cup unsalted butter, at room temperature

$1/2$ cup sugar

2 large eggs

PAN 8-INCH ROUND PAN. PREPARE BY CUTTING A WAX PAPER ROUND TO FIT THE BOTTOM, THEN BUTTERING AND FLOURING BOTH THE PAPER AND THE SIDES OF THE PAN.

1 In a heatproof bowl over simmering water, combine the molasses and coffee, stirring to dissolve the coffee. Remove from heat and set aside.

2 Sift the flour into a bowl, then add the baking powder and salt. Stir to combine and set aside.

3 In a mixing bowl, beat the butter until smooth. Add the sugar and beat until light and fluffy. Add the eggs one at a time, beating well after each.

4 Add the flour and molasses–coffee mixture, beating on low speed just until combined.

5 Spread the batter in prepared pan and bake at 350 degrees for about 25 minutes.

PRESENTATION Frost with Basic Buttercream Frosting (page 98) or Coffee Buttercream Frosting (page 99). Garnish with whole toasted hazelnuts.

CARDAMOM SPICE LOAF

Cardamom, a faintly lemony, faintly peppery spice, is a staple in Scandinavian baking, both in yeast-raised breads and in cakes like this one.

1 cup plus 2 tablespoons all-purpose flour
$1/2$ teaspoon baking powder
$1/2$ teaspoon baking soda
$1/4$ teaspoon salt
$1/4$ teaspoon ground cardamom
$1/2$ teaspoon ground cinnamon
$1/2$ teaspoon ground allspice
$1/4$ cup unsalted butter, at room temperature
1 large egg
$1/2$ cup sugar
$1/4$ cup packed brown sugar
$1/4$ teaspoon vanilla extract
$1/2$ cup plus 2 tablespoons buttermilk
PAN 9 X 5-INCH LOAF PAN, GREASED
AND FLOURED.

1 Measure the flour, baking powder, baking soda, salt, cardamom, cinnamon, and allspice into a bowl and stir to combine.
2 In another bowl, cream the butter until smooth. Beat in the egg, then add the sugars and vanilla and beat until light and fluffy.
3 Mix in one-third of the flour mixture, then half of the buttermilk, beating just until smooth. Mix in the next third of the flour mixture, then the remainder of the buttermilk, and finally the last of the flour, beating each time just until smooth.
4 Pour into prepared pan and bake at 350 degrees for 30 to 35 minutes.

PRESENTATION This loaf is good plain or dusted with a little powdered sugar and cinnamon. It also lends itself to Coffee Buttercream Frosting, Cardamom Cream Cheese Frosting, or Secret Ingredient Pecan Icing (pages 99, 100, and 103).

MARBLE SPICE CAKE

Marble Spice actually arrived on the scene before chocolate marble cakes; when you're in the mood for a mildly spiced cake, this is the one to try.

2 cups sifted cake flour
2 teaspoons baking powder
1/4 teaspoon salt
1/2 cup unsalted butter, at room temperature
1 cup sugar
2 large eggs
2/3 cup milk
1 teaspoon ground cinnamon
1/2 teaspoon ground cloves
1/2 teaspoon ground nutmeg
2 tablespoons light molasses
PAN 8- OR 9-INCH SQUARE PAN, GREASED, AND FLOURED.

1 Combine the sifted flour, baking powder, and salt. Stir to combine and set aside.
2 Cream the butter with the sugar until light and fluffy.
3 Add the eggs one at a time, beating after each addition.
4 Add the dry ingredients alternately with the milk, one-fourth at a time. Beat to thoroughly incorporate after each addition.
5 Pour half of batter into another bowl. To one half of the batter, add the cinnamon, cloves, nutmeg, and molasses.
6 Drop the batter by alternating spoonfuls into the prepared pan. Swirl with a knife or spatula to create a marbled effect.
7 Bake at 350 degrees for approximately 35 minutes.

PRESENTATION Basic Buttercream Frosting (page 98) is excellent with this cake. Since this is a bit larger than most little cakes, double the buttercream recipe and frost the sides as well as the top.

HUMMINGBIRD CAKE

This cake originated in the American South; the editors of *Southern Living* say it's easily their most requested recipe. This version includes coconut, which you may omit.

1 cup all-purpose flour
$2/3$ cup sugar
$1/2$ teaspoon baking soda
$1/4$ teaspoon salt
$1/2$ teaspoon ground cinnamon
1 large egg
$1/3$ cup vegetable oil
$1/2$ teaspoon vanilla extract
$1/3$ cup crushed pineapple with juice
$1/3$ cup chopped pecans plus more for garnish
$1/3$ cup shredded coconut
$1/3$ cup chopped bananas
PAN 8-INCH ROUND PAN, GREASED AND FLOURED.

NOTE This cake should not be beaten. To avoid overmixing, make by hand rather than with an electric mixer.

1 Measure the flour, sugar, baking soda, salt, and cinnamon into a mixing bowl. Stir to combine.
2 Add the egg and oil, and stir just until dry ingredients are moistened.
3 Stir in the vanilla, pineapple, pecans, and coconut. Gently stir in chopped bananas.
4 Pour into the prepared pan and bake at 350 degrees for 25 to 30 minutes.

PRESENTATION The traditional finish for this cake is Basic Cream Cheese Frosting (page 100) garnished with pecans.

TEA CAKES

Nothing is quite so British as the custom of afternoon tea—or is it? Just as tea was drunk in France and Holland decades before it arrived in England, so too was afternoon tea an import from the Continent. In the early years of the nineteenth century, Britons of all classes dined just twice a day. To forestall the fading feeling she got in the late afternoon, the Duchess of Bedford began inviting friends to join her for tea and light refreshments, as she had seen done on the Continent. Small cakes were served at these gatherings, along with sweets and bread-and-butter sandwiches. The custom proved popular and soon it was practiced not only by the upper classes but by the working classes as well.

Although the name implies the opposite, low tea is actually a fancier affair than high tea. High tea, eaten early in the afternoon (when the sun was still near its zenith), became the main meal of the middle and lower classes, with fare consisting of simple, hearty foods such as boiled beef, potatoes, and soup. Low tea, served when the sun had begun to sink, remained an upper-class repast of dainty cakes, pastries, toast points, and pâtés. Although coffee has replaced tea as the favored beverage throughout much of the world, and the leisurely teatime of old is likely to be the hurried coffee break of today, there is an enduring fondness for tea cuisine, of which these recipes are fine examples.

VICTORIAN SANDWICH CAKES

These cakes were among Queen Victoria's favorites and, appropriately, named after her. They can be made from a variety of fresh or leftover cakes—pound and loaf cakes, sponges, and genoise—by cutting thin slices, trimming the crusts, spreading fillings on one slice, and topping with a second slice. Cut the sandwich to a dainty shape or use cookie cutters to make hearts, rounds, diamonds, moons, and stars. Good fillings for sandwich cakes include whipped cream, jam, jelly, fruit puree, cream cheese whipped with honey, or other spreadable frostings.

You can also make Victorian sandwich cakes from homemade Ladyfingers (page 79) by spreading filling on one and topping it with another Ladyfinger, bottom side down. Cut in half to make two dainty sandwiches, and dust with a bit of powdered sugar.

Quick and Easy Teacakes

1 First make one or two of the cake recipes in this book and bake each in an 8- or 9-inch square pan.

2 While the cake is cooling, prepare your frostings. One light-colored frosting, one chocolate, and one fruit glaze will give you a good variety. You can add further variety by dividing the light-colored into two or three batches, leaving one untinted and adding food coloring to the rest.

3 You should also gather a small variety of garnishes—sprinkles, dragees, fresh berries, maraschino cherries and cutouts, fresh flowers, ground cinnamon, nutmeg, cocoa, and grated chocolate are all good choices.

4 When the cake is thoroughly cool, cut into diamonds or squares or use cookie cutters to cut any shape you wish. Now you're ready to decorate. Frost and garnish the top of each little cake, mixing and matching frostings and garnishes to make several different varieties.

ENGLISH TEA CAKES

The English origins of these cakes can be seen in the call for currants, which are smaller and daintier than the California raisins of the U.S. For maximum enjoyment, eat these cakes while reading Dickens, Thackery, or the effervescent Miss Austen.

½ cup dried currants (if you cannot get currants, substitute a like amount of raisins, chopped)

¾ cup all-purpose flour

¾ teaspoon baking powder

¼ teaspoon salt

¼ cup unsalted butter, at room temperature

½ cup sugar

1 large egg

½ teaspoon vanilla extract

3 tablespoons milk

1 teaspoon grated orange zest

PAN MINI-MUFFIN PAN, PREPARED WITH PAPER LINERS OR BY GREASING AND FLOURING EACH CUP. THIS RECIPE WILL MAKE APPROXIMATELY 2 DOZEN MINI-CAKES.

1 Pour boiling water over the currants. Let stand for 10 to 15 minutes, until plumped. Drain and set aside.

2 Measure the flour, baking powder, and salt into a bowl. Stir to combine and set aside.

3 In a mixing bowl, cream the butter. Add the sugar, and cream thoroughly. Add the egg and vanilla, and beat until light and fluffy.

4 Add half of the dry ingredients, then all the milk and the grated orange zest, beating after each addition. Add the remaining dry ingredients and beat thoroughly.

5 Fold in the currants. Fill the cups half full and bake at 350 degrees for 12 to 18 minutes.

PRESENTATION These little cakes can be served without frosting, or with a thin layer of Basic Cream Cheese Frosting (page 100) ornamented with a thin curl of lemon peel.

Hazelnut Tea Cakes

Omit currants and the orange zest. When the batter has been completely mixed, fold in 1/3 cup of ground hazelnuts. Frost with Buttery Chocolate Glaze (page 98).

Cherry Tea Cakes

For two dozen cakes, you will need 12 pitted Bing cherries or 12 maraschino cherries. Cut each cherry in half and let drain on paper towels. Prepare the cake batter as above, omitting the orange zest and currants. After the batter is poured into the cups, place one-half of a cherry into each, cut side down, pressing down so that the batter completely covers the cherry. Like English tea cakes, these can be served on their own, with Basic Cream Cheese Frosting, or with a coating of Pink Glaze (pages 100 and 102).

Cream Cheese Tea Cakes

Omit the currants and orange zest. Cream 1 1/2 ounces of cream cheese – at room temperature - with the butter. Frost with Lemon Cream Cheese Frosting (page 100).

MINIATURE DATE CAKES

We never faced the fruitcake dilemma at Christmas because my grandmother made these delicious little cakes instead. I don't know how old her recipe is, but the fact that it calls for "oleo" (as margarine was once called) suggests that it dates at least to the 1940s. The World War II generation and older baby boomers may remember the fierce wars waged during those years, as the dairy industry applied pressure to keep margarine at a competitive disadvantage. In addition to heavy taxes on margarine, there were also color laws requiring margarine to be sold in its natural, unappealing, lard-like hue. To get around this, manufacturers included a color capsule with each package, which the consumer worked into the margarine herself.

4 ounces pitted, chopped dates
  (about ³/₄ cup)
¹/₂ teaspoon baking soda
¹/₂ cup water
1 tablespoon unsalted butter or
  margarine, at room temperature
¹/₂ cup sugar
1 medium egg
¹/₄ cup chopped pecans or walnuts
¹/₂ teaspoon vanilla extract

³/₄ cup all-purpose flour
¹/₂ teaspoon salt
PAN MINI-MUFFIN PAN, PREPARED WITH PAPER LINERS OR BY GREASING AND FLOURING EACH CUP. THIS RECIPE WILL MAKE APPROXIMATELY 2 DOZEN MINI-CAKES.

1 Place the dates in a small bowl. Sprinkle with the baking soda.
2 Bring the water to a boil. Pour over the dates and set aside to cool.
3 In a mixing bowl, cream the butter and sugar. Add the egg and beat until light and fluffy.
4 Mix in the chopped nuts and vanilla.
5 Mix in the cooled date mixture.
6 Add the flour and salt, and mix until thoroughly combined.
7 Fill the cups half full and bake at 350 degrees for 12 to 18 minutes.

PRESENTATION My grandmother never frosted these cakes but adorned each with half of a maraschino cherry. These cakes are so moist that a cherry half, pressed gently to the cake, will actually adhere. If you prefer frosting, however, top each cake with a dab of Powdered Sugar Glaze or Basic Cream Cheese Frosting (pages 100–101), but don't omit the festive garnish. Besides a half cherry, you may also use a pecan half, walnut, a curl of orange or lemon zest, or a sprinkling of ground nutmeg.

Orange Date Cakes

Reduce the water by 1 tablespoon. When adding the cooled date mixture to the batter, also add 1 tablespoon orange juice and 1 teaspoon grated orange zest. Garnish each with a Candied Citrus Curl (page 91).

Fruit Cake Jewels

If you really can't resist the fruit cake urge, use only half as many dates and add to the Miniature Date Cakes batter enough chopped mixed candied fruit to total about ³/₄ cup.

GINGER BUTTONS

These tender little cakes can be eaten by the handful—unfortunately!

1 cup all-purpose flour
¹/₂ teaspoon baking soda
¹/₂ teaspoon salt
¹/₂ teaspoon ground ginger
¹/₄ teaspoon ground nutmeg
¹/₄ teaspoon ground cinnamon
Pinch of ground cloves
¹/₄ cup molasses
¹/₃ cup hot water
¹/₄ cup unsalted butter, at room temperature
¹/₂ cup sugar
1 large egg

PAN MINI-MUFFIN PAN, PREPARED WITH PAPER LINERS OR BY GREASING AND FLOURING EACH CUP. THIS RECIPE WILL MAKE APPROXIMATELY 2 DOZEN MINI-CAKES.

1 Combine the flour, soda, salt, ginger, nutmeg, cinnamon, and cloves and set aside.
2 Combine the molasses and hot water and set aside.
3 In a mixing bowl, cream the butter and sugar. Add the egg and beat until light.
4 Add one-third of the flour mixture, beating well. Add half of the water and molasses and mix to combine. Repeat, then finish with last third of flour.
5 Fill the cups half full and bake at 350 degrees for 12 to 18 minutes.

PRESENTATION Top each small cake with Orange Buttercream or Lemon Cream Cheese Frosting (pages 99 and 100). I confess my favorite way to eat these is with a dollop of freshly whipped cream dusted with nutmeg. Pure heaven!

PETITS FOURS

Petits fours are the smallest layer cakes in the world, and the most festive little cakes imaginable. They are such a dainty, feminine treat that as I child I thought they'd been invented just for ladies bridge luncheons—"little" treats to serve the "fours" who gathered at the card table. In fact, the name translates to mean "little ovens" and dates back to the 1700s, when baking was an all-day project done on a grand scale. After the larger cakes and breads were made, the ovens took hours to cool down. During this cooling process, bakers probably took advantage of the lingering warmth to use up dabs of leftover batter. Once the little cakes were done, the bakers decorated them to make them appealing, an effort that succeeded so completely that petits fours soon became a sought-after item in their own right.

To make 36 individual petits fours you will need:

1 recipe Genoise, baked in an 8- or 9-inch square pan (page 28).
1 to 4 fillings (see directions).
1 recipe Quick-Set Fondant (page 102).

1 After you have baked the cake and are waiting for it to cool, decide what you want to fill your petits fours with. Almost any frosting or filling that will remain stable at room temperature will work. Avoid whipped cream, for example, and anything that may make your cake too wet, such as fruit syrups. Traditional favorites include buttercream frostings and jam fillings such as Apricot Glaze (page 106). If you want to make all of your petits fours alike, make an entire recipe of an appropriate filling or frosting (pages 95–107). To make four different varieties, you will need one-fourth of each recipe. When the cake is thoroughly cooled and unmolded, and the wax paper has been peeled from the bottom, carefully place it on a cutting board. If the cake still seems too fresh and a bit crumbly, let it dry for an hour or so before continuing.

2 Using a long serrated knife, trim away the edges in the same way you would remove crusts from a slice of bread.

3 Now cut the cake into four equal squares. This will make it easier to work with and will allow you to make four different varieties of petits fours if you wish.

4 Carefully cut each square in half horizontally to make two layers. You may find this easier to do if you hold the square upright in your hand, cupping it gently as you slice downward.

5 Spread the bottom half of each square with the desired frosting or filling. Allow to set 15 minutes before replacing the top layer, cut side down.

6 Using a serrated knife and working with one square at a time, cut each square into three equal strips, then into threes going the other direction, so that each square yields nine perfect little cakes.

7 Arrange the petits fours on a cooling rack that has been placed over a sheet of wax paper. Make Quick-Set Fondant and coat the petit fours as described on page 102.

PRESENTATION Just as an "i" needs its dot, so too do petits fours need a finishing touch. A squiggle of chocolate ganache, a dot of colored frosting, a Maraschino Cutout (page 92), or a tiny piped flower or bow are all good choices. If you wish to add colored sugar crystals, sprinkles, or dragees, remember to do so before the fondant sets, as after it has hardened these adornments will not adhere.

VARIATIONS

You can produce an even wider variety of petits fours by using Chocolate Genoise (page 97) as a base, or by coating your petits fours with a Quick-Set Flavored Fondant or Quick-Set Chocolate Fondant (page 102).

TIP Fondant is extremely sweet and dries to a hard, candy-like glaze. If you prefer a less sugary frosting, ganache can be used instead.

CHOCOLATE MACAROON CAKES

Macaroons well deserve their heavenly reputation—they were invented in a monastery more than two hundred years ago.

For the filling:

1 large egg
1/4 cup powdered sugar
1/2 teaspoon almond extract
1 cup sweetened flaked coconut

For the cakes:

1 ounce unsweetened chocolate
3/4 cup all-purpose flour
Scant 1/2 teaspoon baking soda
1/2 teaspoon salt
2 tablespoons plus 2 teaspoons unsalted
   butter, at room temperature
1/2 cup plus 2 tablespoons sugar
1/2 teaspoon vanilla extract
1/4 cup plus 2 tablespoons milk,
   at room temperature

PAN MINI-MUFFIN PAN, PREPARED WITH PAPER
LINERS OR BY GREASING AND FLOURING EACH
CUP. THIS RECIPE WILL MAKE APPROXIMATELY
2 DOZEN MINI-CAKES.

Make the filling:

1 Carefully break the egg into a bowl. Remove 1 tablespoon of the white and set the rest aside, covered.
2 Combine the tablespoon of egg white with the powdered sugar and almond extract. Mix in the coconut and set aside.

Make the cakes:

1 Melt the chocolate over simmering water and set aside to cool.
2 Measure the flour, baking soda, and salt into a bowl. Stir to combine and set aside.
3 In a mixing bowl, cream the butter until light. Add the sugar, and cream until light and fluffy.
4 Add the remaining portion of the egg with the yolk and beat thoroughly. Add the cooled chocolate and vanilla to butter–sugar mixture.
5 Add half of the dry ingredients, then half of the milk, beating after each addition. Repeat.
6 Fill the cups half full. Top each with a half-teaspoon of filling, pressing the filling down slightly into the chocolate batter. Bake at 350 degrees for 12 to 18 minutes.

PRESENTATION These cakes can be served plain or topped with Buttery Chocolate Glaze (page 98).

ICEBOX CAKES

The fact that we still call them "icebox cakes" says a lot about when and how they became popular. Although cold desserts had long been enjoyed by the wealthy and royal of the world, it was Americans, with their passion for the supernaturally chilly, who brought these treats to the masses.

It all started in the early 1900s, when the primitive icebox of the nineteenth century was replaced by the electric refrigerator of the twentieth. There was just one problem. While the original icebox was a relatively inexpensive necessity, the electric version was an expensive luxury. A 1918 Kelvinator cost $714, about the same as a fridge today— except that back then the average worker's weekly wage was less than $15. To encourage consumers to take the plunge, manufacturers developed elaborate booklets full of tempting recipes that could only be made with the help of the colder, more stable temperatures electricity provided. Although this helped sales, it was not until the postwar prosperity of the late 1940s and early 1950s that ownership became commonplace, and refrigerated desserts—including icebox cakes—became popular. Not only were they glamorously new, but many used packaged foods such as cookies and graham crackers as a base, making baking unnecessary.

Since most refrigerator cakes need to chill overnight, be sure to plan in advance.

STRAWBERRY CHARLOTTE RUSSE

The name of this cake is a corruption of charlyt, an Old English word meaning "dish of custard." Honors for inventing this ethereal dessert actually belong to the legendary French chef Marie-Antoine Carême, chef to both George IV of England and Alexander I of Russia.

Traditionally, charlotte russe was made in a pail-shaped container, lined with strips of sponge cake, filled with custard or Bavarian cream, chilled, unmolded, and decorated with lavish rosettes of whipped cream. In fact, it can be made in any mold available, and adapts well to individual servings.

1 envelope (1 tablespoon) unflavored gelatin
4 tablespoons cold water
1 pint fresh strawberries
½ cup sugar
1 recipe Ladyfingers (page 79), or purchased, sponge-cake style lady fingers.
1 cup heavy cream
PAN 6-INCH SPRINGFORM PAN OR 4 INDIVIDUAL 1-CUP CAPACITY RAMEKINS OR DESSERT CUPS.

1 Place the gelatin and water in a heatproof glass bowl or measuring cup and let soften 8 to 10 minutes. Set the bowl in a saucepan filled with 1 inch of water and warm over low heat, stirring continuously until the gelatin is completely dissolved. Set aside.

2 Clean and hull the strawberries. Slice half of the berries and return to the refrigerator until ready to use. Mash the other half; combine with the sugar in a saucepan and heat until the sugar is dissolved. Remove from the heat, stir in the gelatin, and set aside to cool to room temperature.

3 While the strawberries are cooling, prepare your pan or cups. If you are using individual cups, first line each one with a piece of plastic wrap large enough to overlap the sides—this will make unmolding easier. Line the bottom and sides with ladyfingers cut to the proper length for the sides by trimming the rounded

tip off one end, and standing them upright with the remaining rounded tip pointing up.

4 When the strawberry mixture is cool, whip the cream until stiff. Gently fold in the strawberry mixture, then the remaining sliced berries. Turn the mixture into the pan or cups, cover with plastic wrap, and chill overnight.

5 To unmold, slide a spatula gently around the sides to loosen, then release the springform. If you have made this in individual dishes or a non-springform mold, trim away any bits of cake that rise higher than the filling, then invert onto a serving plate.

PRESENTATION Garnish with additional strawberries or whipped cream.

LADYFINGERS

2 large eggs, separated
$1/8$ to $1/4$ teaspoon almond extract
$1/4$ cup sugar
$1/4$ cup cake flour
1 teaspoon baking powder
PAN A BAKING SHEET LINED WITH PARCHMENT OR WAXED PAPER.

1 Beat the egg yolks until thick and lemon yellow; blend in the almond extract. Set aside.
2 Beat the egg whites until soft peaks form; gradually beat in the sugar until the whites are glossy and very stiff.
3 Fold the egg yolks gently into whites.
4 Sift the measured flour and baking powder over the egg mixture and fold in gently.
5 Place the batter in a pastry bag fitted with a wide plain tip, $1/2$ to $3/4$ inches in diameter.
6 Pipe cookies in oblongs 3 x 1-inch, making shapes as uniform as possible. (If you don't have a pastry bag, you can achieve the same effect by gently dropping the batter from a tablespoon.)
7 Bake at 325 degrees for 5 to 8 minutes, just until the edges turn golden. Cool on a wire rack. Makes about 2 dozen.

TIP If your ladyfingers aren't uniform or if you have burned the edges, don't despair—they can easily be trimmed with the tip of a sharp paring knife.

79

TIRAMISU

Created in the seventeenth century for Cosimo de Medici III, Grand Duke of Tuscany, tiramisu didn't become an international sensation until the nineteenth century. The popular belief that tiramisu derived its name ("pick me up") from Venetian courtesans who ate it to replenish their energy is probably as untrue as it is irresistible. Originally, tiramisu's filling was custard-based, but the modern interpretation, which we offer below, relies on cream and mascarpone cheese.

3 tablespoons water
3 tablespoons honey
$1/3$ cup strong brewed coffee,
    preferably espresso
2 tablespoons brandy, optional
8 ounces mascarpone cheese,
    at room temperature
$3/4$ cup heavy cream
3 tablespoons sugar
1 teaspoon vanilla extract
Purchased crisp (Italian-style) ladyfingers
PAN A SERVING BOWL WITH A 4-CUP CAPACITY.

NOTE If you cannot get mascarpone cheese, cream cheese may be substituted. Crisp, dry ladyfingers are best, but soft sponge-style ladyfingers or strips of sponge cake can be used.

1 Combine the water, honey, and coffee in a saucepan and warm on low heat, stirring, to make a thin syrup. Remove from heat and let cool. Add the brandy, if using.
2 Beat the mascarpone slightly to remove any lumps. Set aside.
3 Whip the cream in a separate bowl, gradually adding the sugar and vanilla, until soft peaks form. Gently fold in the mascarpone.
4 Arrange a layer of ladyfingers to cover the bottom of your serving bowl. Brush or spoon half of the coffee syrup over them. Spread on half of the filling. Add a second layer of ladyfingers and bathe them with the remaining coffee syrup. Cover with the remaining filling. Make sure all of the ladyfingers are evenly covered, and the filling is spread to the edge of the bowl. Cover with plastic wrap and refrigerate 12 to 24 hours.

PRESENTATION Before serving, sprinkle a little cocoa powder over the top.

TRIFLE

Trifle, an English dessert dating from the mid-1700s, evolved as a way to make use of leftover cake that had become too dry to be served again. However, the recipe for leftovers soon proved so popular it became an elegant dessert in its own right, and George Washington is said to have preferred it above all other confections. Traditionally, trifle is served in a footed, straight-sided bowl of clear glass, allowing the happy diners a glimpse of the rich layers of cake, fruit, custard, and cream. However, any pretty glass bowl or serving dish can be used, and trifle can also be made in individual sherbet dishes or even wine glasses. The amounts below are approximate, and can be varied to accommodate the amount of cake you have on hand.

One-layer 8- or 9-inch cake
Sherry (optional)
1 1/2 to 2 cups fresh fruit,
    or 8 ounces frozen fruit (reserve juice)
1 recipe of Vanilla Custard, page 105
3/4 cup heavy cream
2 teaspoons sugar
1/2 teaspoon vanilla extract

NOTES Good fruits for trifle include all varieties of berries (alone or in combination), peaches, nectarines, apricots, cherries, bananas, pineapple, and other full-flavored fruits. Although traditional trifle uses yellow, sponge, or angel food cake, be adventurous and try other combinations. Chocolate cake with cherries or raspberries, gingerbread with pears, and spice cake with pineapple or strawberries are all delicious combinations. If you don't have any fruit on hand, use what trifle makers originally used: jam. A full-flavored berry or apricot jam, spread thinly over each piece of cake, makes a delicious and quick dessert.

1 **To assemble the trifle, slice the cake or break it into chunks. Place half of the cake in the bottom of the bowl and sprinkle with a little sherry or juice from the fruit. Layer with half of the fruit, then spoon on half of the custard. Repeat with the remaining cake, fruit, and custard.**
2 **Whip the cream until soft peaks form. Add the sugar and vanilla and beat until stiff. Spread evenly over the trifle, covering the top completely. Cover with plastic wrap and refrigerate at least 2 hours before serving.**

PRESENTATION Before serving, garnish with additional fruit or slivered almonds.

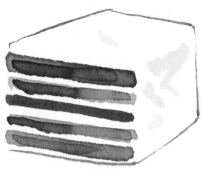

INDIVIDUAL CHOCOLATE WAFER CAKES

Anyone who grew up in America in the 1950s or early 1960s probably remembers this festive cake, one of the most popular back-of-the-box recipes of all time. It still appears on the package of its key ingredient, Nabisco's Famous Chocolate Wafers, although we've heard that these cookies are more difficult to find than they once were. We've included a recipe for the wafers themselves, and the results are definitely worth the extra effort.

For each cake you will need:

¼ cup heavy cream

½ teaspoon sugar

⅛ teaspoon vanilla extract

3 chocolate wafer cookies (Nabisco's Famous Chocolate Wafers, or the following recipe)

1 Beat the cream until it forms soft peaks. Beat in the sugar, then add the vanilla and beat until stiff peaks form.

2 To assemble each cake, spread approximately 1 ½ tablespoons of whipped cream on the bottom of a wafer. Spread evenly, almost to the edges of the wafer. Turn the cookie right side up and place, whipped cream side down, on a flat plate or tray. Press slightly to anchor. Repeat with a second wafer and place it atop the first one, whipped cream side down. Repeat this with a third wafer, so that you have a small three-layer cake. Frost the top and sides with the remaining whipped cream and place in refrigerator overnight.

3 If the cakes have set overnight and if you use a broad, flat spatula, you should have no trouble transferring them to individual serving plates. However, if you're nervous about transferring the cakes intact, make a little extra whipped cream for last-minute repairs or, for easier transferring, build each cake on a disc of wax paper cut slightly larger than the wafer. Don't use a paper doily or other porous paper as a base, as the moisture from the whipped cream will be absorbed by the paper instead of the wafer.

PRESENTATION These cakes look fine unadorned, but you can garnish each with a dusting of cocoa or grated chocolate, a chocolate-coated espresso bean, or half a maraschino cherry that has been thoroughly drained on a paper towel.

CHOCOLATE WAFERS

1 1/4 cups all-purpose flour
1/4 teaspoon salt
1/4 teaspoon baking powder
1/2 cup unsalted butter, at room temperature
1/2 cup sugar
1/2 teaspoon vanilla extract
1 large egg
2 ounces unsweetened chocolate, melted

PAN A COOKIE OR BAKING SHEET, UNGREASED.

1 Sift the flour, salt, and baking powder together and set aside.
2 In a large bowl, cream the butter until light and fluffy. Beat in the sugar and vanilla.
3 In a small bowl, beat the egg lightly with a fork. Add to the butter–sugar mixture and beat well.
4 Add the melted chocolate and mix to combine thoroughly. Add the dry ingredients in thirds, mixing well after each addition. The dough will be quite stiff.

5 Refrigerate the dough 2 to 3 hours, until firm. Roll to 1/8-inch thick on a lightly floured surface and cut with a round cookie cutter, biscuit cutter, or glass rim that is approximately 2 1/2 inches in diameter. Gather the scraps and reroll until all of the dough has been used.
6 Bake on an ungreased cookie sheet at 325 degrees for approximately 8 minutes. Watch the wafers carefully to determine the right baking time for your oven, as you want firm and thoroughly crisp wafers that are not scorched at the edges.
7 After baking, transfer to wire rack and allow to cool thoroughly.

Valentine Wafer Cakes

Add red food coloring to the whipped cream to give a pink glow. Add it a drop at a time, until the right color is achieved. Decorate each cake with a maraschino heart (see Maraschino Cutouts, page 92).

Mint Chocolate Wafer Cakes

Follow the recipe and method for Individual Chocolate Wafer Cakes, but replace the vanilla with a dash of mint extract and a drop or two of green food coloring. This is a perfect dessert for winter holidays, when both green and peppermint are in fashion.

CHEESECAKES

To the victor go the spoils—or at least the cake. According to ancient writings, cheesecake was served to the champion of the first Olympics in 776 B.C.—an appropriate treat since the winner was a cook. Cheesecake's origins probably precede even this early date, and some form of it has probably been eaten since cheese was first made more than 4,000 years ago. And, although the cheese may have been made with goats' milk instead of cows' milk, and sweetened with honey rather than sugar, it probably tasted more like the cake we eat today than any other cake of old.

From Greece the cake made its way to Rome, and the Romans spread the recipe across Europe. It made its way to America in the nineteenth century with the waves of immigrants. Cheesecake's big moment arrived in 1872, when cream cheese was invented, offering cooks across America an inexpensive, reliable, always available new food item. The smooth and silky cheese—richer than its European cousin, Neufchâtel—was ideal for cheesecake, and the dessert table hasn't been quite the same since.

Massive attacks on the nation's dairy supply aren't necessary to make good cheesecake. Ironically, one of the simplest, least expensive recipes I experimented with turned out to be the best tasting. Here it is, adapted from a recipe published on the box of Kraft's Philadelphia Brand Cream Cheese.

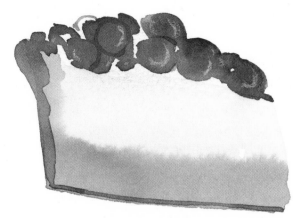

CHEESECAKE

For the crust:

1 cup graham cracker crumbs (7 oblongs
   or 14 2 $\frac{1}{2}$ x 2 $\frac{1}{2}$ -inch squares)
3 tablespoons sugar
3 $\frac{1}{2}$ tablespoons unsalted butter, melted

For the filling:

1 (8-ounce) package of cream cheese,
   at room temperature
$\frac{1}{4}$ cup sugar
$\frac{1}{4}$ teaspoon vanilla extract
1 large egg
PAN 7 $\frac{1}{2}$ OR 8-INCH SPRINGFORM.

Make the crust:

1 Process the graham crackers in a food
processor or place in a heavy-duty plastic
bag and crush with a rolling pin to make
crumbs. Pour the crumbs into the spring

form pan. Add the sugar and stir with fork
to thoroughly blend. Work in the melted
butter with a fork, tossing until the crumbs
are thoroughly moistened and evenly distributed in the pan. With a heavy, flat-bot-
tomed glass, press the crumbs firmly to
form a crust, beginning in the middle
and working out to the edges. Allow some
of the crumbs to come partway up the
sides, using the side of the glass to press
them firm. Set the pan aside.

Make the filling:

1 Lightly beat the cream cheese to make sure
it is smooth and free of lumps.
2 Cream in the sugar and vanilla; add the
egg. Beat to combine thoroughly. Do not
overbeat; you don't want to incorporate
too much air into this batter.
3 Pour into the prepared crust and
bake at 325 degrees for 25 to 30 minutes,
just until set.
4 When the cake is completely cool,
remove the springform ring but leave the
bottom in place. Wrap the cake with plastic
wrap and store in the refrigerator.

PRESENTATION   Aside from a food, the word "cheesecake" can also refer to a pretty woman, scantily clad. That's how I like my cheesecake: scantily clad and dressed only with a garnish of fresh or frozen fruit—preferably strawberries, raspberries, blueberries, cherries, or peaches. If you want a bit more, try one of these toppings:

* A thin layer of sour cream, alone or mixed with honey or pureed fruit, spread over the top
* A fruit glaze (page 106)
* A drizzle of bittersweet chocolate sauce
* Grated chocolate.

NOTE If you don't own a springform pan, use any round 8-inch cake or soufflé dish. Cut waxed paper to fit the bottom, and lightly butter the paper and the sides of the dish. When the cheesecake is done, allow it to cool to room temperature. Run a spatula around the sides and just under the bottom to make sure the cake is loose. Invert onto a plate. Gently peel off the wax paper, then invert again onto the serving plate so the cheesecake is right side up.

Chocolate Cheesecake

For a not-too-sweet chocolate cheesecake, melt 1 ounce unsweetened chocolate. Let it cool to room temperature, and beat with the cream cheese before adding the sugar in the basic Cheescake recipe. For a sweeter, more choco-latey cake, use 2 ounces of semisweet or bitter-sweet chocolate. Serve plain or with a thin coat-ing of sour cream and a garnish of cherries.

White Chocolate Raspberry Cheesecake

After the crust is made in the basic Cheescake recipe, scatter 1 cup fresh raspberries over it. Set aside. Melt 2 ounces of white chocolate. Let it cool to room temperature and beat with the cream cheese before adding the sugar in the basic Cheescake recipe. Finish the batter as described in the basic recipe, pour over the raspberries in the crust, and bake.

Marble Cheesecake

Melt 1 ounce of semisweet chocolate and set aside to cool to room temperature. Make the basic Cheescake, and pour two-thirds of the finished batter into the crust. Add the cooled chocolate to the remaining batter and stir to combine thoroughly. Drop the chocolate mixture onto the poured batter by spoonfuls. Use a table knife to swirl for a marbled effect.

Lemon Cheesecake

After beating the cream cheese in the basic Cheescake recipe, mix in 1 tablespoon of lemon juice, 1 teaspoon of grated lemon zest, and 1 tablespoon of flour. Replace the vanilla with a few drops of almond extract. Finish with a thin layer of sour cream and a garnish of Candied Citrus Curls (page 91).

Peanut Butter Cheesecake

Add ¹/₂ cup plus 2 tablespoons creamy peanut butter to the cream cheese in the basic Cheescake recipe, and cream together. For the ultimate decadence, use a chocolate cookie crust and adorn the top with Chocolate Curls (page 91) or grated chocolate.

Blueberry Swirl Cheesecake

In a saucepan over low heat, warm ¹/₄ cup blueberry jam or fruit puree until smooth and easily spooned. Prepare the cake as described in the basic Cheesecake recipe. Pour half of the batter into the crust. Drizzle on half of the blueberry jam. Spoon on the remaining batter and drizzle with the remaining jam. Gently swirl with a table knife. This variation can also be made with apricot, cherry, raspberry, or strawberry jam.

Individual Upside-Down Pumpkin Cheesecakes

1 Combine the crust ingredients from the basic cheesecake recipe in a bowl. Divide equally among 6 individual, lightly buttered ramekins. Press firmly with a glass to form the crust.

2 Prepare the filling as in the basic Cheesecake recipe. After the egg has been added, add 5 tablespoons of canned pumpkin, ¹/₂ teaspoon of ground cinnamon, ¹/₄ teaspoon of ground cloves, and a pinch of ground ginger. Mix thoroughly to combine. Divide the batter among the ramekins.

3 Fill a 9 x 13-inch cake pan with 1 inch of water. Place the ramekins in the pan and bake at 325 degrees for approximately 25 minutes, just until set. Remove the pan from the oven, but leave the ramekins in it for 10 minutes. Remove the ramekins and let set another 10 to 15 minutes. Run a spatula around the sides to loosen, then invert each cake onto an individual serving dish and serve upside down. These are wonderful warm or cold, with a bit of whipped cream spiced with ginger. This recipe can also be made in a traditional springform pan and served right side up.

FROSTING 101

Small cakes are the opposite of the towering confections that show off their icings like models strutting down a runway. Too much frosting will overwhelm a small cake, not only aesthetically but taste-wise. You don't want your cake to look overdressed, nor do you want to bury its homemade taste in too much frosting. But that doesn't mean your cake should be a plain Jane. This chapter is filled with ideas and recipes for frostings and fillings that will dress your little cake to perfection.

Unless otherwise stated, the frostings in this book make enough to ice the sides and top of an 8-inch round cake or the top of an 8- or 9-inch square cake. I often don't frost the

sides of my little cakes at all, and when I do I use only a thin layer, just enough to seal the cake. More, I find, can easily become too much of a good thing. If you want to cut your cake into two layers and fill it with a layer of frosting, please double the frosting recipe.

Now, to get down to the business of applying the frosting. First, you need something to apply the frosting with. I have a small metal spatula I like, but you can also use an ordinary butter knife. Unless a recipe specifies otherwise, always begin with a cake that has cooled completely. It is easier to work with, less fragile, and less likely to shed crumbs. If you are going to divide the cake into two layers, do that first; spread the frosting or filling of your choice to within $1/2$ to $1/4$ inch of the edges. Replace the top, pressing down slightly to make sure it is firmly attached. Now you're ready to do the top and sides.

Conventional wisdom usually calls for doing the top first, then the sides. I do it in the reverse order, and I don't think it makes a great deal of difference. What does matter is how much frosting you put on your knife or spatula. Many people can't resist scooping up a big, lavish glob and plopping it on the cake. But doing this means you will have to drag a lot of that lavish glob over the cake to get it evenly distributed. Not only is this time-consuming and messy, you run the risk of tearing and damaging your cake.

If you are working on the sides of the cake, take a small amount of frosting (less than a tablespoon) and smooth it gently onto the sides, working in both directions. Turn the cake to the next bare spot and spread more frosting, working backward to join the part you have already frosted, and forward. Repeat until you have worked all the way around the cake.

To frost the top, I usually apply a very thin layer first to act as a crumb coat. Then I ladle the rest of the frosting on in several blobs and spread it evenly. Of course, some of the frosting lops off the edge, which is desirable if I've left the sides bare. If I've already frosted the sides, it's easy to touch up those spots to give the cake a finished look.

DRESS IT UP!

In addition to frosting, there are all sorts of embellishments you can add to your cake. Here are some favorites:

Spatula Play

If you don't plan to garnish your cake, you can use your butter knife or spatula to embellish the frosting by making either myriad small swirls or large, spoke-like swirls that radiate from the center; finish by scraping the frosting from the spatula into a tiny, tempting little dollop to set in the middle of the cake, and top with a single nut or cherry. You can also make little peaks all over the cake by pressing the tip of the knife or spatula flat against the frosting, then lifting straight up to "pull" the frosting. If the spatula bores you, go to the drugstore and buy an inexpensive wide-toothed comb—it's great for etching squiggly lines on your frosting. You can also buy a gadget called a "cake comb" which does the same thing and doesn't cost very much more.

Piping

Even if you can't make a sugar rose or roll fondant to save your life, you can still give your cake a professionally decorated look. All you'll need is a recipe of Decorator Icing (page 96), a pastry bag or piece of parchment folded into a cone, and a few basic decorator tips, such as a plain round tip, a star, and a ribbon. Use half the icing to frost the cake, then tint the rest with food coloring (or leave it as is). Fill the pastry bag and pipe a border around the top or bottom edge of the cake, then cover the top of the cake with the motif of your choice. One of the easiest shapes to make, using a plain tip, is a simple little spiral. A cluster of three dots is equally easy and a cake scattered with these clusters takes on an invariably cheerful look. If you have some ornamental tips, try making little stars, rosettes, or flowers. Every motif needn't be perfect—it's the overall effect that counts, and a guest who is truly troubled by a squidgy bit of stray frosting should not be invited back.

Sprinkles & Dragees

These come in a greater variety of shapes, colors, and sizes than ever before. You can get simple, cheerful varieties in almost any grocery store, or go online or to a cake supply store and get the most sophisticated of shapes and shades, including some I've seen that look like colored metallic beads. I use both the simple and sophisticated, depending on the cake and the occasion. One of the most useful types to get is the large (8mm) white pearl ball, which can be arranged around the top edge of a cake to make a beaded border. You can also arrange balls on top of the cake in clusters to suggest flowers, snowflakes, swags, and swirls.

Drizzling

Chocolate sauce in a squeeze bottle can be a cake baker's best friend, and makes an especially pleasing display on white frosting. You can either drizzle some on free-form, or try a more elegant pattern. On a round cake, apply chocolate in narrow concentric rings at intervals of about an inch. Use a table knife to lightly draw eight radiating spokes from the center of the cake to the outer edge, so that the knife pulls the chocolate into a ripple pattern. On a square cake, drizzle a series of parallel bars, then pull the knife top-to-bottom on one row, bottom-to-top on the next to create a herringbone pattern.

Dusting

Somewhere in your cupboard you have the makings of an elegant cake garnish. If you've made a spice cake with, for example, a cream cheese frosting, sprinkle a little cinnamon or nutmeg over the top. If you've frosted your devil's food cake with white icing, try a dusting of cocoa powder, or try a sprinkling of colored sugar.

Colored Sugar

Yes, you can spend the equivalent of $20 a pound on colored sugar crystals, as I once did, or you can make your own, as I later learned to do. To make your own, you need a heavy-duty (freezer weight) zip-lock plastic bag. Put a few heaping spoonfuls of sugar in the bag, along with a few drops of food coloring. Seal the bag and work the food coloring into the sugar with your fingers. Keep working until the color is evenly distributed and the sugar is free of clumps. Not only will you save money, but you'll be able to make a far wider and more sophisticated spectrum of colors than is usually available at the store.

Stenciling

The easiest way to enhance an unfrosted cake is to lay a paper doily over the top and sift on some powdered sugar, leaving a pretty pattern when the doily is removed. This works especially well on spice cakes and chocolate cakes, whose dark color shows the powdered sugar off to good advantage. Doilies aren't the only templates you can use, though. If you've decorated your home with stencils, you may have a template with a usable motif on it—just use masking or painters tape to cover over the part of the stencil you don't want to use. Or, if you or your children have paper punches that make snowflakes, hearts, stars, or any of dozens of other shapes, you can make your own templates with them.

Ribbon

If you don't wish to frost the sides of your cake, try cutting a length of wide ribbon to circle the cake. You can use a bit of icing to secure the ends or a straight pin, making sure

to remove and discard it when the cake is cut. Great for gift cakes.

Chocolate Curls

There's no trick to these elegant-looking adornments—I make mine with an ordinary potato peeler and a block of good quality chocolate. I have found, however, that you get a better curl if you warm the chocolate with your hand for a few seconds before you start. Don't place your palm directly against the chocolate, but have a piece of foil or wax paper in between. Hold your palm against the chocolate for just about 10 seconds. Then grab the chocolate block by the other end and run your peeler along the warmed edge. Curls can be made out of dark, milk, or white chocolate.

Candied Citrus Curls

These colorful spirals, reminiscent of party ribbons, look elegant but are quite easy to make. This method will work for lemons, oranges, and limes, and the only "special" equipment you need is an ordinary vegetable peeler. This recipe is enough for 1 orange, 1 lemon, or 2 limes.

With the vegetable peeler, remove the peel from the fruit in thin strips, taking only the colored part and avoiding the white. With a sharp paring knife, scrape off any pith or membrane from the inner side of the peel, and cut the strips into matchstick-sized pieces. Place in a small saucepan; add water just to cover. Bring to a boil and boil for 30 seconds. Drain the strips. Rinse and dry the saucepan. Return the strips to the saucepan, along with 2 tablespoons of water and 4 tablespoons of sugar. Heat to a simmer, stirring to dissolve the sugar. Continue stirring over medium heat until the strips are translucent and the syrup has thickened, about 20 minutes. When the curls are done, drain them well on paper towels. These can be made ahead and kept, covered and at room temperature, for up to 24 hours.

Toasted Coconut

Place approximately $1/3$ cup sweetened shredded coconut in a skillet. Toast over medium heat, stirring frequently, until the coconut is light golden brown and slightly crisped. Store covered at room temperature.

Dipped Strawberries

Fresh strawberries that have been partially dipped in melted white or dark chocolate and allowed to set make a temptingly beautiful garnish for almost any cake.

Strawberry Fans

Start with a large, fresh strawberry that has been rinsed clean and patted dry. Strawberries with stems left on are best. Do not hull. Make several slices by cutting vertically almost to, but not through, the stalk end, so that the slices are still attached. Press the stalk end gently to make the slices fan out.

Frosted Fruit

Mix water with meringue powder according to the package instructions. Use a small paintbrush to coat fruit. Sprinkle with granulated white sugar to give a frosted look. This works best with smooth, fairly firm fruit such as grapes, blueberries, and the like.

Nuts

Pecans, walnut halves, and hazelnuts not only dress up a cake, they can provide cutting guidelines. If, for example, you want your cake to yield eight servings, place nut halves on top of the cake at 12 o'clock and 6 o'clock, then 3 o'clock and 9 o'clock. Place additional nut halves between each of these marks. Cut each slice with the nut as a center marker, and you will get eight perfectly equal pieces of cake. If you want to make your cake look a bit fancier, use a dollop of frosting or whipped cream as a base for each nut.

Maraschino Cutouts

One of the best investments you can make is in a set of aspic cutters. These handy utensils, like miniature cookie cutters, are designed to cut jellied aspic shapes to adorn pâtés, canapés, and the like. However, their uses are multiple: they can be used to create lacy cutouts in rolled cookies, for example, or to make pastry shapes with which to decorate pie crusts. They are also, I've discovered, excellent for cutting fancy shapes from maraschino cherries.

Aspic cutters come in a variety of styles and sizes: leaves, stars, hearts, teardrops, diamonds, and so on, and a set of cutters measuring $1/2$ or $3/4$ inches each is ideal for making small decorations. To cut shapes from maraschino cherries, drain each cherry well, then cut in half. Nick each end slightly to make the cherry easier to spread. Place it skin-side down on a cutting board, flatten slightly, and cut with the shape of your choice. Press firmly to make sure the cutter has cut all the way through the cherry skin. Use a bamboo skewer to loosen and remove the decoration from the cutter. Shapes can be cut ahead of time and stored in the refrigerator, covered, until ready for use.

Edible Flowers

If you have a garden, you can grow your own cake decorations. Nothing looks sweeter on small cakes than a drift of blossoms. Just make sure to avoid any blooms you don't absolutely know are safely edible; never use plants that have been sprayed with insecticides or other chemicals, or that come from a florist.

Common edible flowers include the following: apple blossom, carnation, chive blossom, clover, dianthus, gardenia, geranium, hibiscus, hollyhock, honeysuckle, impatiens, jasmine, lavender blossom, lemon verbena, lilac, mint, nasturtium, orange blossom, pansy, peach blossom, plum blossom, rose, snap dragon, squash blossom, violet.

FROSTINGS AND FILLINGS

WHIPPED CREAM

Whipped cream is by far the most versatile cake accessory. You can use it as a frosting or filling, or serve it on the side to make any cake more lavish. It's delicious plain, and can be flavored in any number of ways. Just remember: any cake that has a whipped cream frosting or filling must be stored in the refrigerator.

1 cup heavy cream
1 to 2 tablespoons sugar
$1/2$ teaspoon vanilla extract

1 The best bowl to make whipped cream in is metal, as it chills quickly and retains the cold. Glass and crockery are acceptable,

plastic less desirable, and wood the worst choice of all.

2   At least an hour or more before whipping the cream, place both the bowl and the beaters in the refrigerator. (If you're pressed for time, set them in the freezer for 15 minutes.) If you have just come home from the grocery store with your cream, it also will need time to chill—at least a few hours, and preferably longer.

3   If you are whipping cream by hand, fill a larger bowl with ice water, and set your mixing bowl in it while you work. If possible, however, whip cream with a handheld electric mixer—it's much easier and you won't need to bother with the ice-water setup.

4   Begin on low speed and beat for about 30 seconds, until small bubbles appear. Increase the speed to medium and beat another 30 seconds, then increase to high speed. Be sure to move the beaters around in the bowl and to scrape the sides with a spatula to make sure all the cream is being whipped.

5   When the whipped cream gains volume and the beaters begin to leave soft trails, add the sugar and flavoring. If you are making whipped cream to serve on the side, add 1 tablespoon of sugar. If you intend to use it as a frosting or filling, add 2. Continue to whip as you add ingredients, and scrape sides frequently.

6   Beat until cream doubles in volume and forms firm peaks. When it does this, stop. Some people think that the stiffer cream is beaten, the longer it will hold up, but this isn't true. Overbeaten cream is more likely to separate and collapse, and loses the creamy delicacy that makes it special.

NOTE Leftover whipped cream that has gone flat can usually be rescued. Chill it in a mixing bowl in the refrigerator for 2 hours or in the freezer for 30 to 45 minutes. Chill the beaters as well. Rewhip without adding any additional ingredients.

Chocolate Flecked Whipped Cream

After the cream is whipped, gently fold in $\frac{1}{2}$ cup grated bittersweet or semisweet chocolate.

Chocolate Whipped Cream I

In a heavy saucepan, combine 1 cup heavy cream and 6 ounces of chopped semisweet chocolate. Warm over low heat, stirring constantly, until the chocolate melts. Transfer to a metal bowl and refrigerate until thoroughly chilled, at least 2 hours. Whip the cream following the basic method above, but do not add additional sugar or flavoring.

Chocolate Whipped Cream II

Use the basic recipe (above) but increase the

sugar to $1/4$ cup and add 2 tablespoons plus 1 $1/2$ teaspoons of unsweetened cocoa powder.

Chocolate Chocolate Chip Whipped Cream

After making Chocolate Whipped Cream I or II (above), fold in $1/2$ cup of mini chocolate chips.

Crème Chantilly

Whip the cream as in the basic recipe (page 93) replacing the vanilla with 1 tablespoon of amaretto, Kahlúa, or the liqueur of your choice.

Mocha Whipped Cream

In a heavy saucepan, dissolve 2 teaspoons of instant coffee powder in 2 tablespoons of boiling water. Add 4 ounces of chopped semisweet chocolate and 1 cup of heavy cream. Warm over low heat, stirring constantly, until the chocolate melts. Transfer to a metal bowl and refrigerate until thoroughly chilled, at least 2 hours. Whip the cream following the basic method (page 93), but do not add additional sugar or flavoring.

Raspberry Whipped Cream

Sprinkle 1 cup of fresh raspberries with 2 teaspoons of sugar. Crush lightly with a fork and set aside. Whip the cream as directed in the basic recipe (page 93), replacing the granulated sugar with 2 tablespoons powdered sugar and decreasing the vanilla to 1/4 teaspoon. Drain the raspberries, reserving their juice. Gently fold in the berries and 1 teaspoon of the juice.

Strawberry Whipped Cream

Clean 1 cup fresh strawberries. Slice thin, sprinkle with 1 tablespoon of sugar, and set aside. Whip cream as directed in the basic recipe (page 93), replacing the granulated sugar with 2 tablespoons of powdered sugar. Drain the strawberries, reserving their juice. Gently fold in the berries and 1 teaspoon of the juice.

LADY BALTIMORE FROSTING

This is a basic boiled frosting, which was the frosting of choice until the early 1920s, when American-style buttercreams gained ascendancy. For a true trip to nostalgia land, try it on Lady Baltimore Cake (page 19), or on any other cake you choose.

1 cup white sugar
2 tablespoons plus 2 teaspoons water
2 tablespoons light corn syrup
Pinch of salt
2 large egg whites
$1/4$ teaspoon cream of tartar
$1/2$ teaspoon almond extract

1 In a heavy saucepan, combine the sugar, water, corn syrup, and salt. Stir over medium heat until the sugar dissolves. Stop stirring and bring up to 240 degrees (until a bit dropped in

water forms a soft ball, and syrup trails off the spoon in a thin thread).

2 As the syrup is heating, beat the egg whites until soft peaks form. Add the cream of tartar and beat until stiff peaks form.

3 When the syrup reaches the desired temperature, pour it into the egg whites in a thin stream, beating continuously. Add the almond extract and beat until the frosting is fluffy and spreadable.

WHITE DECORATOR ICING

This makes enough to frost and decorate a one-layer cake. Leftover frosting may be frozen.

$3/4$ cup unsalted butter, at room temperature
2 cups powdered sugar
1 tablespoon water
$1 1/2$ teaspoons light corn syrup

1 Beat the butter until light. Gradually mix in half of the powdered sugar, then the water and corn syrup, and finally the remaining powdered sugar. Beat until smooth and creamy.

2 Frost the cake. If you wish, add food coloring to tint the remaining icing. Load into a pastry bag fitted with a tip and decorate the cake as desired.

BASIC VANILLA FROSTING

$1/4$ cup unsalted butter, at room temperature
$1 3/4$ cups powdered sugar

$1/2$ teaspoon vanilla extract
1 to 2 tablespoons milk

1 Cream the butter until light. Gradually beat in the powdered sugar. Add the vanilla.

2 Add the milk a little at a time, beating until light and fluffy and the frosting reaches spreading consistency.

Brickle Chip Vanilla Frosting

Mix in $1/2$ cup of chopped pieces of chocolate-covered buttercrunch, such as Skor, Heath Bar, or Daim.

Coconut Pecan Vanilla Frosting

Mix in 1/2 cup of shredded coconut and 1/2 cup of pecans, broken in pieces.

Maraschino Cherry Vanilla Frosting

Replace the milk with maraschino cherry juice, and mix in 2 tablespoons of drained, chopped maraschino cherries. If you want pinker frosting, add a drop of red food coloring.

Swirl Vanilla Frosting

Swirl in $1/4$ cup of jam such as strawberry, raspberry, blackberry, or blueberry.

BASIC CHOCOLATE FROSTING

$1/4$ cup unsalted butter, at room temperature
3 tablespoons unsweetened cocoa powder

1 ½ cups powdered sugar
½ teaspoon vanilla extract
2 ½ to 3 tablespoons heavy cream or milk

1 Cream the butter with the cocoa powder until fluffy. Gradually beat in the powdered sugar. Add the vanilla.
2 Add the cream a little at a time, beating until light and fluffy and the frosting reaches spreading consistency.

Chocolate Mint Frosting

Replace the vanilla with a little peppermint extract. I've found that this extract varies greatly in strength from brand to brand, so the best way is to add a few drops, then taste. This is the hard part of being a cook.

Chocolate Mocha Frosting

Replace the milk with cold, strong coffee.

LAVISH FUDGE FROSTING

People especially love fudge frosting, so this recipe makes extra. If you have leftover, spread some between graham crackers, sandwich-style.

2 ounces unsweetened chocolate
¼ cup unsalted butter, at room temperature
2 cups powdered sugar
¼ teaspoon vanilla extract
1 ½ to 2 tablespoons heavy cream or milk

1 Melt the chocolate over simmering water. Set aside to cool to room temperature.
2 Cream the butter until light and fluffy. Gradually beat in the powdered sugar.
3 Add the cooled chocolate and vanilla and mix until thoroughly combined.
4 Add the cream a little at a time, until the desired spreading consistency is reached.

CHOCOLATE GANACHE

8 ounces semisweet or bittersweet chocolate
1 cup heavy cream

1 Chop the chocolate very fine, or pulse in a food processor. Set aside.
2 In a heavy saucepan, bring the cream just to a simmer. Remove from the heat and add the chocolate, stirring until it is melted and smooth.
3 Scrape the mixture into a bowl and chill in the refrigerator, stirring occasionally, until thick enough to spread. (This will take 2 to 4 hours.) If the ganache becomes too thick, remove it from the fridge and let it soften at room temperature.

White Chocolate Ganache

Make Chocolate Ganache using white chocolate instead of semisweet.

White Chocolate Mint Ganache

Add peppermint extract to taste to White Chocolate Ganache. Start with a drop or two and increase as desired.

BUTTERY CHOCOLATE GLAZE

$3/4$ cup heavy cream

3 tablespoons unsalted butter

1 tablespoon plus 1 teaspoon sugar

$1/2$ teaspoon vanilla extract

9 ounces semisweet chocolate, chopped

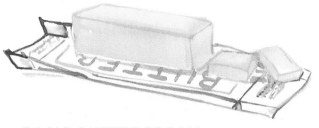

1 In a heavy saucepan, heat the cream, butter, and sugar until the butter melts and the sugar dissolves. Stir constantly and do not let the mixture boil.

2 Remove from the heat and add the vanilla and chopped chocolate. Stir continuously until the chocolate has completely melted and the mixture is smooth.

3 Let cool at room temperature, stirring occasionally, until thick enough to spread, about 1 hour. If the mixture becomes too thick, or if you wish to make it ahead of time and refrigerate until ready for use, warm it gently over low heat until spreadable.

TIP Here's an easy way to melt chocolate over hot water without worrying about getting water in the chocolate. Place a metal colander in the pan of simmering water, making sure the water rises high enough to cover the colander's bottom but not more than halfway up the sides of the colander. Now you can set the heatproof bowl with your chocolate in the colander without worrying that it will capsize.

BASIC BUTTERCREAM FROSTING

$1/2$ cup unsalted butter, at room temperature

$3/4$ teaspoon vanilla extract

$1 1/2$ cups powdered sugar

$1 1/2$ to 3 tablespoons milk

1 Cream the butter until smooth.

2 Add the vanilla and one-third of the powdered sugar. Beat until smooth.

3 Add another third of the powdered sugar. Beat until smooth.

4 Beat in 1 tablespoon of milk. Add the remaining powdered sugar and beat until smooth and fluffy. Beat in additional milk, 1 teaspoon at a time, until the desired consistency is reached.

Chocolate Buttercream Frosting

Cream the butter with 5 tablespoons of unsweetened cocoa powder, and increase the vanilla to 2 teaspoons. This frosting will require 3 tablespoons of milk.

Coffee Buttercream Frosting

Omit the vanilla. Use 2 tablespoons of hot milk in which you have dissolved 2 rounded teaspoons of instant coffee powder. Let cool to room temperature before using.

Lemon Buttercream Frosting

Replace the milk with freshly squeezed lemon juice, and mix in $1/2$ to 1 teaspoon of grated lemon zest.

Maple Buttercream Frosting

Replace the milk with 3 tablespoons of maple syrup. If you wish, add 3 to 4 tablespoons of finely chopped walnuts or pecans.

Orange Buttercream Frosting

Replace the vanilla with $1 1/2$ teaspoons of grated orange zest. Replace the milk with orange juice.

WHITE CHOCOLATE BUTTERCREAM FROSTING

3 ounces white chocolate, chopped
2 tablespoons heavy cream
$1/2$ cup unsalted butter
$1/2$ cup powdered sugar

1 Melt the chocolate in the cream over simmering water, stirring continuously. Set aside and let cool to room temperature.
2 Cream the butter until light. Gradually beat in the sugar, then the cooled chocolate, beating until the frosting is smooth, light, and fluffy.

White Chocolate Almond Buttercream

Make as White Chocolate Buttercream, adding $1/8$ to $1/4$ teaspoon of almond extract as you are beating in the cooled chocolate. To finish, mix in $1/4$ cup chopped or slivered toasted almonds.

WHITE CHOCOLATE MERINGUE FROSTING

While raw egg whites do not pose a great risk of salmonella, they are not risk-free, and the American Egg Board advises against consuming any raw egg products. I have made this classic recipe using meringue powder, with good results every time.

$2 1/2$ ounces white chocolate, chopped
$1/2$ cup unsalted butter, at room temperature
1 large egg white or equivalent prepared
   from meringue powder
$1/4$ cup superfine sugar
2 to 3 drops almond extract

1 Melt the chocolate over simmering water, stirring continuously. Set aside.
2 Beat the butter until light and creamy.
3 In a separate bowl, beat the egg white or rehydrated meringue powder until soft peaks form. Gradually add the sugar, beating until the meringue is stiff and glossy.
4 Beat the butter into the meringue in four parts, beating until smooth after each addition. Your

meringue will initially lose its silken gloss and you may think you have ruined your frosting. You haven't, and the mixture will eventually regain its luster.

5 After the butter has been incorporated, add the cooled white chocolate and almond extract, and beat until smooth and thoroughly blended.

Chocolate Meringue Frosting

Make as White Chocolate Meringue Frosting, substituting 2 ounces of semisweet chocolate for the white chocolate and $1/4$ teaspoon of vanilla extract for the almond extract.

BASIC CREAM CHEESE FROSTING

For an 8-inch round cake:

$1/2$ cup butter

4 ounces cream cheese

$1 1/3$ cups powdered sugar

$1/4$ teaspoon vanilla extract

Bring both the butter and cream cheese to room temperature and cream until light. Gradually add the powdered sugar, then the vanilla. Beat until smooth and fluffy.

Almond Cream Cheese Frosting

Replace the vanilla with $1/4$ to $1/2$ teaspoon of almond extract.

Cardamom Cream Cheese Frosting

Add $1/4$ teaspoon of ground cardamom to start, and a little more if you want a stronger flavor.

Chocolate Chip Cream Cheese Frosting

Stir $1/2$ cup of mini chocolate chips into the frosting.

Chocolate Cream Cheese Frosting

Melt 3 ounces of semisweet chocolate, cool to room temperature, and beat into the frosting.

White Chocolate Cream Cheese Frosting

Melt 3 ounces white chocolate, cool to room temperature, and beat into frosting.

Lemon Cream Cheese Frosting

Add 1 tablespoon of lemon juice and 1 teaspoon of grated lemon zest or, if you have it, 2 tablespoons of lemon curd.

Strawberry Cream Cheese Frosting

Mix $1/4$ cup of mashed ripe strawberries into the frosting.

TIP To bring cream cheese to room temperature quickly, place it in a freezer-weight zip-lock bag or a waterproof plastic container, and submerge in a bowl of warm water.

GRAPEFRUIT FROSTING

4 ounces cream cheese
1 tablespoon minced fresh grapefruit
2 teaspoons grapefruit juice
$1/2$ cup powdered sugar

Bring the cream cheese to room temperature and beat until smooth and light. Mix in the minced grapefruit, then add the grapefruit juice and beat until blended. Gradually beat in powdered sugar.

NOTE This frosting can be a bit runny on a warm day. If so, set the bowl in the refrigerator a few minutes before frosting your cake or, if you like a sweeter frosting, beat in a little extra powdered sugar.

POWDERED SUGAR GLAZE

1 cup sifted powdered sugar
$1/2$ teaspoon vanilla extract
1 to 2 tablespoons of milk, depending on desired thickness

Place the powdered sugar in a small bowl. Add the vanilla and 1 tablespoon of milk. Beat until smooth and add more milk until the desired consistency is reached.

Almond Glaze

Replace the vanilla with $1/4$ to $1/2$ teaspoon of almond extract.

Apple Cider Glaze

Omit the vanilla. Replace the milk with apple juice or apple cider and add a dash of cinnamon.

Coffee Glaze

Omit the vanilla. Dissolve 2 rounded teaspoons instant coffee powder in 2 tablespoons of hot milk. Let cool, then beat into the powdered sugar.

Lemon Glaze

Omit the vanilla. Use 2 tablespoons of lemon juice instead of milk.

Orange Glaze

Omit the vanilla. Use 2 tablespoons of orange juice instead of the milk and add $1/2$ teaspoon grated orange zest.

Pineapple Glaze

Omit the vanilla. Use 2 tablespoons of pineapple juice instead of the milk.

Pink Glaze

Replace the vanilla with $1/4$ to $1/2$ teaspoon of almond extract. Use maraschino cherry juice instead of milk.

Spice Glaze

Replace the vanilla with 1 teaspoon of apple pie seasoning (or $3/4$ teaspoon of ground cinnamon and $1/4$ teaspoon of ground cloves).

QUICK-SET FONDANT FOR PETIT FOURS

3 cups powdered sugar
$1/4$ cup water
1 teaspoon vanilla extract
1 tablespoon light corn syrup

1 Combine all the ingredients in bowl and stir until you have a smooth, stiff paste.
2 Scrape the fondant into a heavy saucepan and heat on low, stirring constantly. The fondant will begin to thin. When it becomes translucent and thin enough to pour, spoon it over petits fours, making sure the glaze runs over the top and down the sides. Use the back of a metal spoon or a butter knife to push and smooth fondant to cover the sides completely. Since this fondant sets up quickly, you will need to keep it hot while you work, either by reducing the heat to a holding warmth, or by resting it in a pan of hot water. If the fondant cools and begins to stiffen, it can be reheated at any time.

On the other hand, if the glaze was too thin when you poured it, you can repeat with a second coat. After the petits fours have set, scrape up the bits of hardened fondant that dripped onto the wax paper and save for reheating. Covered and stored in the refrigerator, fondant of this type will last for weeks.

NOTE Fondant can be colored any shade you wish using food coloring.

Quick-Set Flavored Fondant

You can add subtle flavor to this fondant by replacing the vanilla with other flavored extracts such as almond, lemon, orange, or peppermint.

Quick-Set Chocolate Fondant

Melt 2 ounces of unsweetened chocolate and set aside. Proceed as in the basic recipe, but add an extra tablespoon of water. When the fondant is heated, stir in the melted chocolate. Since fondant is extremely sweet, you do not need to increase the amount of powdered sugar.

BROWNED BUTTER FROSTING

$1/4$ cup unsalted butter
2 cups powdered sugar
1 teaspoon vanilla extract
2 to 3 tablespoons milk
1 Place the butter in a saucepan over medium heat and melt, stirring constantly, until the butter foams and just begins to turn golden,

about 5 or 6 minutes. Be careful not to let the butter burn.

2 Remove from the heat and transfer to a mixing bowl.

3 When the butter has completely cooled, add the powdered sugar and vanilla and beat on medium speed. Gradually add enough milk to give the desired spreading consistency.

BUTTER PECAN ICING

2 tablespoons unsalted butter

$1/4$ cup chopped pecans

1 tablespoon maple or pancake syrup

1 cup powdered sugar

1 tablespoon milk

In a small pan, melt the butter over low heat. Add the pecans and toast lightly, stirring frequently. Transfer to a bowl and stir in the syrup. When the pecan mixture has cooled to room temperature, mix in the powdered sugar and milk.

SECRET INGREDIENT PECAN FROSTING

$1/2$ teaspoon instant coffee powder

4 ounces cream cheese, at room temperature

1 tablespoon milk

$1 3/4$ cups powdered sugar, sifted

$1/2$ cup chopped toasted pecans

1 Add the coffee powder to the cream cheese and beat until light and creamy.

2 Add the milk, then gradually add the powdered sugar, beating continuously.

3 If the frosting seems too thin, add a bit more powdered sugar. If it is too stiff, add a bit more milk, $1/2$ teaspoon at a time to avoid overthinning.

4 When the frosting is the desired consistency, mix in the pecans.

COCONUT PECAN FROSTING

$1/4$ cup unsalted butter

$1/2$ cup firmly packed brown sugar

$1/4$ cup evaporated milk

$3/4$ cup flaked sweetened coconut

$3/4$ cup pecans, broken in pieces

1 Combine the butter, brown sugar, and evaporated milk in a saucepan over low heat. Heat, stirring, until the butter melts and the sugar dissolves.

2 Remove from the heat and stir in the coconut and pecans. Spread over the cake while the frosting is still warm.

PEANUT BUTTER FROSTING

1 tablespoon unsalted butter,
   at room temperature
2 tablespoons creamy style peanut butter
1 1/2 cups powdered sugar
2 to 3 tablespoons milk

1 Beat the butter and peanut butter
together until fluffy.
2 Sift in the powdered sugar a third
at a time, beating after each addition.
3 Mix in enough milk to bring
frosting to spreading consistency.

PENUCHE FROSTING

3 tablespoons unsalted butter
1/4 cup firmly packed brown sugar
2 teaspoons milk
1/2 cup powdered sugar
1/2 cup flaked sweetened coconut, toasted

1 In a saucepan, melt the butter over low heat.
Add the brown sugar and stir until it has melted
and combined with the butter. Add the milk 1
teaspoon at a time.
2 Bring to boil, stirring constantly. When the
mixture begins to bubble, remove from the heat.
3 Scrape into a bowl and allow to cool
10 minutes.
4 Blend in the powdered sugar.
5 Frost the cake while the frosting is still warm.
Garnish with toasted coconut.

CARAMEL ICING

1/3 cup sugar
1 cup packed brown sugar
2/3 cup milk
2 teaspoons unsalted butter
1/2 teaspoon vanilla extract

1 Combine the sugars and milk in a heavy
saucepan over medium-high heat. Bring to a boil,
stirring constantly. When the mixture reaches
236 degrees (the stage at which a bit dropped in
water will form a soft ball), remove from heat.
2 Add the butter and vanilla, stirring until the
butter melts and is thoroughly combined.
3 Let cool to lukewarm, then beat until creamy
and spreadable.

VANILLA CUSTARD FILLING

To use in Trifle (page 81); more than enough for a 9-inch cake:

1/2 cup sugar

1 1/2 tablespoons cornstarch

3 eggs

1 1/2 cups milk

1 teaspoon vanilla extract

1 In a heavy saucepan, combine the sugar and cornstarch.

2 In a separate bowl, beat the eggs lightly, then whisk into the saucepan. Stir in the milk.

3 Heat over low to moderate heat, stirring continuously. Be careful not to have the heat too high, or the custard may curdle or scorch. When the mixture has thickened (4 to 5 minutes), remove from heat and stir in the vanilla. To ensure a smooth, creamy custard, continue stirring until cool.

BING CHERRY FILLING

1 (15 1/2-ounce) can dark sweet cherries

1 tablespoon cornstarch

2 tablespoons kirschwasser or other liqueur

1 Drain the cherries, reserving liquid.

2 In a saucepan, whisk together the cornstarch and 2/3 cup of the reserved cherry liquid. Add the cherries and cook over medium heat, stirring, until the mixture has thickened and begins to bubble.

3 Cook 2 more minutes, stirring constantly. Stir in the liqueur.

4 Remove from the heat. Cover and let cool to room temperature before using.

SOUR CHERRY FILLING

2 cups pitted fresh pie (sour) cherries

1/2 cup plus 2 tablespoons sugar

2 tablespoons cornstarch

2 teaspoons unsalted butter

1/4 teaspoon almond extract

Toss the cherries with the sugar and let stand for 15 minutes. Scrape into a saucepan, place over medium heat, and stir in cornstarch. Bring to a boil, stirring constantly, then lower the heat and simmer just until the juice becomes a translucent syrup. Remove from the heat and stir in the butter and almond extract. The filling will become thicker as it cools. Bring to room temperature before using.

BLUEBERRY FILLING

2 cups fresh blueberries, cleaned and picked over 1/4 cup plus 2 tablespoons sugar

1 tablespoon plus 1 1/2 teaspoons cornstarch

Pinch of salt

1/2 cup water

1 1/2 teaspoons unsalted butter

1 Place 1/2 cup of the blueberries, the sugar, cornstarch, and salt in a saucepan. Toss to coat

the blueberries. Add the water and cook over medium heat, stirring frequently, until thick, about 10 minutes.

2 Remove the saucepan from the heat, stir in the butter, and let stand 5 minutes.

3 Scrape into a bowl, stir in the remaining blueberries, and chill in refrigerator.

LEMON CURD FILLING

$1/4$ cup plus 1 tablespoon freshly
     squeezed lemon juice
$1 1/2$ to 2 teaspoons grated lemon zest
     (to taste)
$1/4$ cup plus 2 tablespoons sugar
2 large eggs
Pinch of salt
$1/4$ cup unsalted butter, cut into small pieces

In a heavy saucepan over low heat or in a heatproof bowl over simmering water, combine lemon juice, lemon zest, sugar, eggs, and salt. Whisk to combine. Add butter, stirring continuously. Heat until the curd thickens and the first bubbles appear. Transfer to a bowl and cover by pressing plastic wrap directly onto the surface; this will prevent a skin from forming. Chill before using.

LEMON SYRUP

$1/2$ cup sugar
$1/2$ cup lemon juice

1 Bring the sugar and lemon juice to a boil, stirring constantly to dissolve sugar.

2 Remove from heat. Let cool before using.

Orange syrup

Replace lemon juice with orange juice.

APRICOT GLAZE

In a heavy saucepan, gently warm 1 cup of apricot jam. Press the warmed jam through a sieve and spread immediately on the cooled cake. This method can be used with a variety of other jams, as a glaze or as filling between layers.

SPICED APPLE TOPPING

Fruit toppings are a quick way to perk up a plain cake, and go particularly well with yellow cakes, pound cakes, gingerbread, and nut cakes. Don't forget to add a rosette of whipped cream as well.

2 medium apples (chose a frim cooking
     or baking variety)
2 tablespoons unsalted butter
2 tablespoons packed brown sugar
1 to 2 teaspoons ground cinnamon, to taste
$1/2$ teaspoon ground nutmeg
1 tablespoon lemon juice

1 Peel, core, and dice the apples into $1/4$-inch pieces.

2 Melt the butter in a small skillet. Add the
diced apples and sauté over medium heat,
stirring frequently, until the apples are soft,
about 5 minutes. Reduce the heat and add the
sugar, cinnamon, nutmeg, and lemon juice,
stirring to coat the apples. Turn off the heat,
cover, and keep warm until ready to use, or
make ahead of time and gently reheat.

Spiced Peach Topping

Use 2 fresh peaches in place of the apples
and add $1/4$ teaspoon ground ginger.

Spiced Pear Topping

Use 3 small fresh pears in place of the apples.
Omit the nutmeg and add $1/4$ teaspoon of
ground ginger.

Spiced Pineapple Topping

Use 1 to 1 $1/4$ cups drained pineapple chunks
in place of the apples, and 1 tablespoon
of the pineapple juice instead of the lemon
juice. Omit the nutmeg. Spice with 1 teaspoon
of ground cinnamon, and $1/2$ teaspoon of
ground allspice.

INDEX